READING REVOLUTION

Shakespeare on Robben Island

READING REVOLUTION

Shakespeare on Robben Island

Ashwin Desai

UNISA PRESS • PRETORIA

enclassed, ... from awe, worship, degree, ... himself; just, gentle, wise; but man ... unless? – no, yet free from guilt or pain.

L. T.

© 2012 University of South Africa
First edition, first impression

ISBN 978-1-86888-683-8

Published by Unisa Press
University of South Africa
P O Box 392, 0003 UNISA

Project editor: Lindsey Morton
Editor: Na-iem Dollie
Book design & typesetting: Andri Steyn
Printer: Harry's Printers

Telephone: 086 12 DALRO (from within South Africa); +27 (0)11-712-8000
Telefax: +27 (0)11-403-9094
Postal Address: P O Box 31627, Braamfontein, 2017, South Africa
www.dalro.co.za

Every effort has been made to trace copyright holders or use works in the public domain. We apologise for any inadvertent omissions, and will correct such errors if pointed out.

CONTENTS

This *Complete Works of Shakespeare* was covered in plastic. It was carried off Robben Island by former political prisoner Marcus Solomon, who was incarcerated in the general section of the prison.

PREFACE

Shakespeare winged this way using other powers

to wrest from grim rock and a troubled student-lad

an immortality outlasting all our time

and hacking out an image of the human plight

that out-endures all facets of half-truth:

here now we hurtle north-east from the westering sun

that follows, plucks out from afar

the wingstruts crouched and sunlit for a plunge:

O might I be so crouched, so poised, so hewed

to claw some image of my fellows' woe

hacking the hardness of the ice-clad rock,

armed with such passion, dedication, voice

that every cobblestone would rear in wrath

and batter down a prison's wall

and wrench them from the island where they rot.

— Dennis Brutus, 1970, Robben Island prisoner

Robben Island. An island rock in the icy waters of the Atlantic Ocean off Cape Town. For many long days, months and years, prisoners were pressed together on this bleak stretch of ground, breaking stones by day and harried and hurried into bare cells by night.

If there was any relief from the tedium and toil, it was reading. Under the guise of continuing their education, the constant eye of the censor and the struggle over bureaucracy and pettiness, the political prisoners of Robben Island received a trickle of books.

This book is about those books. It tells the story of how the classic texts of European literature were devoured by prisoners who sought to change society and who now, cut off from the world and starved of news of contemporary life, had only the travails of Julius Caesar or Caliban upon which to reflect.

> 'Exploded?' said the Queen … The young man said security may have thought it was a device. The Queen said: 'Yes. That is exactly what it is. A book is a device to ignite the imagination.' (Bennett 2007:14)

Travelling across the country and meeting some of the very first anti-apartheid saboteurs, leaving the single cells and entering the world of the communal block, the stories became more intriguing, the range of books more diverse and a whole history of resistance to apartheid began to take shape.

Through the single cells of Robben Island, a copy of *The Complete Works of Shakespeare* did the rounds and forms the centre-piece of this intriguing and inspiring story. It was every bit as holy to me as the *Book of Kells*, that battered Shakespeare placed in my hands by island inmate Sonny Venkatrathnam. It was a *Complete Works* that had sections signed by some of the most well-known luminaries in the struggle against apartheid: Nelson Mandela, Govan Mbeki, Neville Alexander, Ahmed Kathrada, Strini Moodley, Walter Sisulu …

In many accounts of the island, the fact that there were two sections to the prison is often lost. The single cells, which comprised up to 30 prisoners and where, among others, the Rivonia triallists were incarcerated. And the general section, whose history is under-written and where as one inmate recounts 'treatment was harsh and barbarous. The warders inflicted corporal punishment on us at will … It was the nearest thing to an omnipresent hell on earth' (Mogoba 2004:33).

The commitment to studying and the desire for basic literacy in the general section especially opened up new worlds to all those condemned to lengthy absences from society. Some freedom fighters were 'illiterate' when they arrived on the island but, during moments snatched from the roving eye of prison warders, they came to read and write their first letters, learning the alphabet on sand and slates spirited away from the quarry of hard labour. In these cells, prisoners copied out books in long

hand and in relays deep into the night, as time ticked quickly for the books' return to libraries in far away universities.

Although the sections were sealed off from each other, the inmates were communicating across the walls and barbed wire through literature.

Dennis Brutus left the island in July 1965. Shakespeare arrived, 'winging' his way into the single cells but also into the communal cells. Rather than rotting, inmates used literature and the spread of literacy to re-imagine the prison.

Former inmate Marcus Solomon still has a copy of *The Complete Works of Shakespeare*. Covered in plastic, it was one of the few books that Solomon carried off the island:

> Most of the books we had used for our studies we left there for use by those remaining. We brought back the books we had wanted for ourselves for some reason or the other. I brought the *Shakespeare* and three other books: *Collected Poems of W. B. Yeats*, given to me by Dennis Brutus when he left the island; *A History of Southern Africa* by Eric A Walker, which I had found extremely useful while studying history; and *The Rise and Fall of the Third Reich* by William Shirer.

There are fading quotes at the back end of the book. From T. S. Eliot, Leon Trotsky and from Shakespeare's *Much Ado About Nothing*: 'What need the bridge much broader than the flood?'

The PAC's Robert Mangaliso Sobukwe, who lived Lear-like in a house cut off from every other political prisoner on the island, was reading Howard Fast's *My Glorious Brothers* and *Spartacus* and Arthur Koestler's *Darkness at Noon*. He drew the line at Ian Fleming, telling Benjamin Pogrund, 'I fail to see what makes the books bestsellers; but perhaps it is because I haven't seen the pictures. There is a violent revolution taking place in European society, don't you think? With literature coming down from the head and skirts coming up from the knees' (Pogrund 2009:247).

The Rivonia triallist Ahmed Kathrada, serving a life sentence, was reading *Spartacus* at the same time, marking off a quote:

there are certain categories of human beings who do not welcome the light of day. A prisoner hugs the night, which is a robe to warm and protect him, and daylight brings no cheer to a condemned man. But most often, daylight washes out the confusions of the night. (Venter 2005:37)

For Sobukwe, *My Glorious Brothers* spoke more powerfully to him than *Spartacus*. 'My wife and I read it together, page by page from beginning to end. And we wept as we read' (Pogrund 2009:247). Nelson Mandela devoured Tolstoy's '*War and Peace* in three days …' (Sampson 1999:286). Given the poverty of resources, reading could not be systematic. But still reading was often linked to political debates. Sobukwe read Arthur Koestler's *Darkness at Noon* twice and it 'provided him with ammunition to fight the Reds' (Pogrund 2009:247).[1]

In a prolonged debate over the *Freedom Charter*, Neville Alexander and Nelson Mandela returned to their single cells and sought material to buttress their arguments. In the communal section, Sedick Isaacs recalls how prisoners were often hesitant to return books if 'they thought the book was too critical of their organisation's ideology or their opposite' (Isaacs 2010:63).

In the early years, from 1964 onwards, there were debates across organisational boundaries in the communal cells. Much of the debate between ANC and PAC members revolved around the nature of the Soviet Union, whether it was 'communist or socialist or practicing some form of "state capitalism" ' (Isaacs 2010:108). There were also debates around race, with the ANC accusing 'the PAC of being chauvinistic as well as racist because they only admitted people who were Black as members … The PAC … pointed out that the ANC's policy of multi-racialism actually amounted to "racialism multiplied"' (Isaacs 2010:108). These open debates declined as they became increasingly acrimonious and were replaced with a form of 'political education', held within the confines of the various organisations.

As communication between single and communal sections improved, debates permeated the walls, even if they were often inside political camps:

Was the armed struggle's objective to force the ruling class to the negotiating table about the seizure of power? Was the Freedom Charter designed to bring about a 'bourgeois democracy' or as the Communists asserted 'the Freedom Charter represented the workers and the oppressed, confronted by the white capitalist class'? (Sampson 1999:291)

Reading and discussions occurred against a backdrop of Soviet Marxism that ran strongly through the prison walls. This was a Marxism of rigid formulas that pre-empted debate rather than stimulating it. Sometimes the walls got higher but just as often they came falling down. Between the imposed discipline and silence there was the noise of intellectual and political contestation and growth.

This world stood in stark contrast to that of the warders. They seemed stuck in time. Imprisoned in a world that saw them as innately superior. As the prisoners read books and debated issues of the day and graduated with university degrees, the warders' response was, 'You can have a 101 doctorates but you are a kaffir … you are a number … you are nothing' (Tshwete, quoted in Schadeberg 1994:39).

With the devotion to learning plainly apparent among prisoners, some of the warders took up studying, enrolling for degrees similar to those of their charges. However, it was the men they locked up at night who were destined for far, far more.

Superficially, Shakespeare is part of a Eurocentric canon that crowds out valuable and more relevant black and female voices. It is high brow, alienating and Shakespeare's elevation as the epitome of literature is part of the way in which white supremacy assigns value to its cultural artefacts above those of the 'empire's periphery' (Saul 2008).

However, a solid body of work exists that reveals not only a subversive Bard but also a justifiable celebration of the excellence of his work, to which not only the English are heirs but all artists. Throughout the 1950s, *The Tempest* became a touchstone for anti-colonial struggles, as writers such as George Lamming, Edward Brathwaite and Aimé Césaire sought to rewrite Caliban into history. Thus Césaire wrote:

To me Prospero is the complete totalitarian. I am always surprised when others consider him the wise man who 'forgives'. What is most obvious, even in Shakespeare's version, is the man's absolute will to power. Prospero is the man of cold reason, the man of methodical conquest – in other words, a portrait of the 'enlightened' European ... Caliban is the man who is still close to his beginnings, whose link with the natural world has not yet been broken ... Caliban is also a rebel – the positive hero, in a Hegelian sense. The slave is always more important than his master – for it is the slave who makes history. (Quoted in Nixon 1987:571)

As I turned the pages of the *Complete Works*, sure enough, Billy Nair, who spent twenty years on the island, had marked off a section from *The Tempest*:

CALIBAN:

This island's mine ...

... and here you sty me

In this hard rock, whiles you do keep from me

The rest o' the island.

Act I, Scene 2

If the situation on Robben Island – where enemies of a social system were sustained by the very literature upon which that system's claims to natural superiority was based – is not a cautionary tale, then nothing is. The message to despots is that no end of suppression will deny an idea (or a Caliban) whose time has come. Aspirations to freedom and dignity are acclaimed in literature everywhere.

Books and plays often had a different pull on prisoners with many of their accounts giving us a deep sense of reading as 'rewriting the text of the work within the text of our lives' (Barthes, quoted in Scholes 1989:10). While Sobukwe was reading texts that gave him 'ammunition' to debate the communists, imprisoned liberation fighters from rural areas could identify with the John Steinbeck's *Grapes of Wrath*. They were witness

to apartheid's gobbling of land held in common for generations and the forced march of entire villages of men into wage labour in far off urban centres. Mandela realised:

that Tolstoy was more interested in aristocrats than in the common people, but he enjoyed his jibes against them ... and he would partly identify with General Kutuzov, who allowed Napoleon to capture Moscow but this encompassed his defeat, and who understood the Russian soul. (Sampson 1999:286)

These stories about books, that as often as they were read were turned upside down, is a fascinating encounter with the generation that was so crucial in ushering in South Africa's democracy. The central research approach taken in this book is to rely on open-ended questions focused on developing life histories, what Goodson has called life politics (2006). This was especially directed to understanding what prisoners first 'brought' to Robben Island in terms of education and knowledge of literature, and how they responded to the books and general intellectual environment while incarcerated. This allowed an approach that follows Scholes's *Protocols of Reading* in which he argues that 'Both texts and readers are already written when they meet, but both may emerge from the encounter altered in some crucial respect' (1989:92). In selecting the prisoners there was a deliberate attempt to cut across political divides and that of the 'single' and 'general' sections of the prison. The book is divided into eleven chapters. The first chapter provides a background into the struggles that prisoners engaged in to obtain reading material, develop educational classes and to broaden the opportunities to pursue formal studies. The following nine chapters present the lived experiences of the prisoners.

The concluding chapter attempts to speak to the time of the Calibans in power. *The Tempest* lost a lot of resonance as it became evident that the promises of the national liberation struggle, 'where all things would be held in common and Nature would provide "all foison, all abundance" for the "innocent people" ' was an optimistic reading (Maslen & Schmidt 2008:199). As Nixon puts it, '*The Tempest*'s value for African and

Caribbean intellectuals faded as the plot ran out. The play lacks a sixth act …' (1987:576).

This was the period of neo-colonialism, when independence was circumscribed and many erstwhile Calibans began to behave like Prospero:

> as Fanon rightly observes, nationalist consciousness can very easily lead to frozen rigidity; merely to replace white officers and bureaucrats with coloured equivalents, he says, is no guarantee that the nationalist functionaries will not replicate the old dispensation.

> The dangers of chauvinism and xenophobia … are very real. It is best when Caliban sees his own history as an aspect of *all* subjugated men and women, and comprehends the complex truth of his own social and historical situation. (Said 1994:258)

What then of the record of South Africa's Calibans in power? Have those traditions, honed on the island, come to seize those who command political authority? How and why do we dispose of our own Caesars, and resist the urgings of rank ambition by our own witches and wizards cooking up cauldrons of toil and trouble?

XI

ACKNOWLEDGEMENTS

The financial support of SANTRUST is gratefully acknowledged. A special thanks to Dr. Anshu Padayachee, CEO of South Africa-Netherlands Research Programme on Alternatives in Development (SANPAD) who believed in this book from the start. Ashwell Adriaan provided outstanding support with regard to research and interviews. Joanne Rushby and Na-iem Dollie did more than edit. Lindsey Morton from UNISA Press was incredibly supportive. Andri Steyn was a brilliant designer of the book and never allowed sharp deadlines to threaten her creativity. Finally, and most importantly I am indebted to the Robben Islanders who gave so freely of their time.

Grateful thanks are also due to a number of publishers and individuals for permission to use covers, pages, etc, as illustrations, as follows:

William Shakespeare: The Complete Works (edited by Peter Alexander). Cover and pages reprinted by permission of HarperCollins Publishers Ltd © 1951.

The Tudor Shakespeare (edited by Peter Alexander). Cover reprinted by permission of HarperCollins Publishers Ltd © 1951.

A Prisoner in the Garden: Opening Nelson Mandela's Prison Archive. Photograph of Sedick Isaacs courtesy Nelson Mandela Centre of Memory.

Time Longer Than Rope: A History of the Black Man's Struggle for Freedom in South Africa, by Edward Roux © 1964 the Board of Regents of the University of Wisconsin System. Cover reprinted courtesy of The University of Wisconsin Press.

The Iron Heel, by Jack London. Cover reprinted by permission of Penguin Books Ltd © 1945.

The Grapes of Wrath, by John Steinbeck. Cover reprinted by permission of Penguin Books Ltd © 1951.

'Our University' struggle poster, original drawing by Ken Sprague, reproduced by courtesy of the Ken Sprague Fund.

Indian Delights: A Book of Recipes by the Women's Cultural Group (edited by Zuleikha Mayat), reproduced by courtesy of the Women's Cultural Group © 1976.

Nanima's Chest, by Zuleikha Mayat, reproduced by courtesy of the Women's Cultural Group © 1981.

Acknowledgement is made of Shutterstock images used in this book

Thanks to Jurgen Schadeberg for permission to use photos taken in 1994.

Thanks to Rüdiger Wölk, Münster, for permission to use his photos on Wikimedia Commons.

Thanks to Rajesh Jantilal, photographer of some of the portraits in this publication, and of the annotated pages of *William Shakespeare: The Complete Works*.

John Steinbeck

The Grapes of Wrath

BK.

PENGUIN MODERN CLASSICS   5/-

John Steinbeck's *The Grapes of Wrath* was widely read by liberation fighters imprisoned on Robben Island.

Robben Island watch tower (Photo by Jurgen Schadeberg, 1994).

INTRODUCTION

Away with him, I say! Hang him with his pen

And inkhorn about his neck

Henry VI, Part 2; Act IV, Scene 2

The stories that follow take place in the context of a notorious prison, which was not only designed to incarcerate but also to brutalise and break inmates both physically and psychologically.

Steve Tshwete, who was incarcerated for twelve years on the island, remembers warders shouting, 'A kaffir is a dog and you are a dog' (quoted in Schadeberg 1994:39). Govan Mbeki, serving a life sentence, writes of the fact that warders did not regard the prisoners 'as normal human beings' but 'as a deadly enemy which had to be destroyed', although he wryly adds, 'I don't know if it would be correct to say that they even regarded us as animals because they cared a lot for their animals' (quoted in Schadeberg 1994:29). Neville Alexander, who spent ten years on the island, reveals that the warders 'had a zoological perspective on prisoners and treated us all like that' (Lodge & Nasson 1991:302).

What the stories in this book reveal is the way prisoners confronted their situation. It is remarkable to know that on Robben Island the zoological specimens were reading Shakespeare. They were also reading John Steinbeck, Jack London and Leon Trotsky. Mandela preferred Tolstoy to Dostoyevsky and 'read Dickens and the English poets, including Wordsworth, Tennyson and Shelley … He also read biographies of … several Boer War generals … While the Afrikaner government was accusing Mandela of being a communist, he was studying not Marx but their own heroes' (Sampson 1999:286).

Marcus Solomon, who spent 10 years on the island from 1964 to 1974, remembers:

> I have never read so much in my life. In fact, I stopped reading novels for quite a while after the island. I read every major novel. (Interview, March 2011)

By 1978 the Cape Provincial Library had opened a depot with some 2 500 books. 'Things were looking up, and the desire to read on the island was palpable' (Sisulu 2004:417).

There were ironies.

On the one hand, prisoners with their quest for knowledge and on the other, the warders of the master race, armed with a crass brutality and anathema to knowledge.

Many ironies.

None starker than while being baited by warders that they would rot in jail, prisoners sought to obtain degrees and prepare for the future. Those who were free, the prison authorities, generally could not be bothered with reading and studying, believing in a god-given superiority that saw black people as hewers of wood and drawers of water.

In 1970 the subsidy covering half of the tuition fees of the prisoners was ended. One of the reasons it was rumoured to be happening was that

> the prison authorities were beginning to be extremely unhappy about the intellectual disparity between prisoners and warders. This disparity was growing rapidly and wider every day. (Dingake 1987:177)

Sometimes the lack of education and knowledge of the warders was a bonus. For example, Fikile Bam remembers how Neville Alexander was able to get 'both volumes of Deutscher's *The Prophet Armed* and *The Prophet Unarmed*', while a right-wing book because it had the word 'communism' was banned (Lodge & Nasson 1991:302).

Aubrey du Toit, who started working as a warder on Robben Island in 1976, remembers that one of his

> duties included censoring the study material and films as well as outgoing assignments. I had no official training for this and sometimes I didn't know what I was looking for. For instance you as a warder know nothing about political science, and yet you had to censor political science assignments. I remember I had to censor Andrew Mlangeni's assignments. He was an honours student in political science. Looking back I think it was a joke for an Afrikaner with Standard 10 to censor these difficult assignments. (Quoted in Schadeberg 1994:47)

Out of apartheid's gulag emerge the most incredible stories of prisoners reading, studying and supporting others in that quest. The stories in this book traverse both the single and communal cells, and are sensitive to the different challenges faced. As Eddie Daniels, who spent 15 years on the island, attests, the single cell environment, which housed about 30 prisoners 'was extremely claustrophobic' and 'any friction, tension or anxiety among prisoners was aggravated by this proximity with one another' (Daniels 1998:191). It was a section in which you had a number of people with high levels of formal education. So at any one time there was Neville Alexander with a doctorate, Fikile Bam, a degree, Andrew Masondo, a mathematics lecturer at Fort Hare, Lesley van der Heyden, a high school English teacher, Pascal Ngakane and Masla Pather, both medical doctors. There was also a strong leadership core in the single cells with access to resources.

In the communal cells the challenges were different. Many of the prisoners arrived without much education. Political contestations could take violent forms. Exercising discipline was harder. The warders meted out beatings with impunity.

Sedick Isaacs arrived on the island in 1965. He recounts the experience he had of a whipping by a warder. He was strapped to a flogging machine, called a 'merry', and was kept in isolation for eleven months and had almost a year added to his sentence.

Isaacs provides a window into the challenges faced by the fact that up to thirty per cent of prisoners could not read or write. Therefore, one of the most important tasks was to start a literacy programme. But also there was a need to have discipline in cells housing up to 50 people. In the study cell, C1, he recounts:

> Somebody clapped his hands and quiet descended over the cell. It was study period ... An hour later the same person clapped his hands to signify the study period was over and conversation started again ... At eight o' clock the bell rang to tell prisoners that they must now sleep. Only those with study privileges were allowed to stay awake till ten o' clock when a warder would come and flick the lights to indicate it was time to sleep. I once asked a warder what the charge would be if I did not sleep. His simple answer was that 'Jy sal jou gat sien' (You will see your arse). (Isaacs 2010:64)

2

When Isaacs was released from prison he made a living from selling eggs. Somehow he returned to studying and finished a doctorate, becoming head of Informatics at Groote Schuur Hospital in Cape Town. We will hear from him and his amazing journey later in the book.

In the beginning was the Book

> Aung Min chose his words carefully. 'I want you to tell me about your friends there (prison)' ... The boy talked about his lizard, and the beetle in the box, and the great Tan-see Tiger ... 'And books,' he said. 'My friends were books.' (Connelly 2008:9)

Michael Dingake arrived on Robben Island in 1966. Twenty-one years later he published *My Fight Against Apartheid,* chronicling his 15-year imprisonment on the island. While Dingake spent much of his incarceration in the single cell section, his book stitches together the debates on the island that ran from ideology, to the nature and form of resistance inside prison, to the everyday lives of the prisoners. As Dingake recounts, there were many restrictions placed on those who pursued formal study. For example, students were not able to lend their books to non-students, nor were they able to lend books to one another even if they were studying the same subject (Dingake 1987:72). In addition, prisoners could only have their studies paid for by their families. These two conditions 'meant that only those who had adequate funds could enjoy the privilege reasonably and be in a position to sit for examinations' (Dingake 1987:172).

> These conditions made it impossible for those prisoners who could not afford to buy books or whose families could not afford their fees to study. For political prisoners deeply committed to an egalitarian society, this was an outrage. (Sisulu 2004:283)

The inmates debated whether these study conditions should be accepted, given the restrictions. It was settled in favour of acceptance as prisoners, especially those who were serving long sentences, felt they needed to keep their minds alive in an environment that cut them off from the outside world and sought to deny them any form of intellectual stimulation. But there were more issues at play than just the restrictions on who could study. The prisoners had to overcome many hurdles placed in their path by the prison authorities. By 1967, Dingake was studying towards a BA:

> Although the University of South Africa enrolls students from October, students from Robben Island never registered earlier than February. The excuse was that normally those who had written exams

Most guards had a modicum of schooling, and yet they were often put in charge of vetting literature sent to political prisoners. (Photo: Jurgen Schadeberg, 1994.)

The general section of the prison also had communal work areas. In the picture prisoners are cutting wood. (Photo: Jurgen Schadeberg, 1994.)

> at the end of the year could be given permission to register with the University before their results were known. The results were usually received around Christmas. But permission, which had to be sought every year, was never forthcoming until the end of January. The point is that every year the Robben Island students registered late by four months or more. (Dingake 1987:173)

Already starting months behind other students, the process was exacerbated by the fact that study materials and books may not even arrive at all.

> You might make an application to a South African library for a book on contract law. They would process your request and then send you the book by post. But because of the vagaries of the mail system, the remoteness of the island and the often deliberate slowness of

censors, the book would reach you after the date by which it needed to be returned. If the date had passed, the warder would typically send the book back without even showing it to you. Given the nature of the system, you might receive a late fine without ever having received the book. (Mandela 1994:398–399)

The cells did not have stools or tables, 'except a square piece of slanting masonite secured to the wall by brackets. One had to stand and do one's reading and writing' (Dingake 1987:174). As Stanley Mogoba ironically comments, 'It is not surprising that the pass rate was high. One could not fall asleep easily, and one's concentration was always high!' (Mogoba 2004:43).

Prisoners found ways to improve conditions from time to time. Over a protracted period, Dingake and some fellow prisoners built themselves bookshelves:

> Whenever we worked by the seaside we made it a point to collect some useful flotsam, planks mainly, for construction of our bookcases. It depended on the disposition of the warder in charge on the particular day. The next day a not so well disposed warder could not only refuse permission to bring any planks into the section, he might dismantle anything constructed already and charge the prisoner for unauthorized possession. (Dingake 1987:175)

The worst years on Robben Island were from 1962 to 1966, but after a hunger strike there was an improvement. By the end of the 1960s, privileges around learning were trimmed again. Postgraduate studies and undergraduate studies in history, law and political science were banned. Those who already had prior permission, and therefore exemption from the banning, were subjected to all kinds of actions designed to make it as difficult as possible to study. These new strict developments coincided with the arrival of Colonel Badenhorst. During his tenure, 'all legal procedures and processes in gaol administration' were suspended (Dingake 1987:177). One of the most debilitating moves made by Badenhorst was to downgrade prisoners from a C to a D category.

> The downgrading had a thoroughly demoralising effect on the prisoners because it meant automatic loss of certain privileges, the

4

number of letters they could write and the visits they could receive. Worst of all, those who dropped from C to D grade were not entitled to the study privilege. (Sisulu 2004:321)

In the general section, Sedick Isaacs's final BA examination became a disaster:

> The university regulations required that the third-year courses must be sat and passed together. As was required by the Prison Department I had to apply for a day off from the Quarry for each examination. The Commanding Officer of Robben Island, in his wisdom decided that a D group prisoner like Sedick Isaacs must not be allowed to be absent so often from work in the Quarry. Leave of absence from work in order to write examinations was given for two out of the six papers … No amount of complaining could change this decision. (Isaacs 2010:160)

The departure of Badenhorst witnessed an improvement, but the enforcement of petty rules and vindictiveness continued. Sifiso Buthelezi arrived on Robben Island in 1986 at the age of 24. He registered for a Bachelor of Commerce degree. He remembers how:

> a comrade accidentally came across a pile of unreturned library books in the dustbin. We had borrowed these books from the UNISA library and the study office was meant to post them back. They punished the comrade who brought this matter to the attention of the authorities and withdrew his study privileges. (Buthelezi, quoted in Schadeberg 1994:59)

While the island of Buthelezi's time was a different world from the harshness and brutality that marked the early years, when Dingake and others fought daily battles to create a space to read and write, it was still marked by vindictiveness.

The prison of thought

> The whites would try to deny us to study … Because it is this education, it is the very education that made us to stand up against the whites … If you are uneducated, people would push you from one side to that side because you don't know who you are, you don't

know your rights, ja. Whites were trying to deny us, but we insisted … you see that this is what one warder Richard, he was from Pretoria … he told us that 'manne, if we give you education, you are sharpening the spear against us'. (Alcott Dumelelo Blow, a prisoner on Robben Island from 1963 to 1969)

This insistence on learning and the desire for knowledge could not be contained. The formal avenues for study were only one aspect of how prisoners sought out an education. Even places meant to be punishing, such as the lime quarry, became sites of inspiration and sharing.

The ability to conduct classes 'while swinging a pick or shoveling lime' was developed over time (Alexander, quoted in Lodge & Nasson 1991:301). As Fikile Bam remembers:

> Just about anybody who had a degree or any form of education was allocated a subject to teach. Every morning … before going to work, the teachers would come together quickly and discuss their programme for the morning as to which periods would follow which

---

The limestone quarry on Robben Island where political prisoners held lessons while working. (Photo: Rüdiger Wölk, Münster)

Robben Island as seen from Table Mountain.

at the workplace … So there was always movement when you got to the workplace, little groups assembling in different places, and you knew that there were classes in progress. This is really how the whole process started; so that by the time the authorities were prepared to give us formal permission to study – after we had applied for it – with outside institutions, this structure of teaching was always on the ground. (Bam, quoted in Lodge & Nasson 1991:301)

The island was a place where sometimes teachers met their former students. When Stanley Mogoba was a teacher at Kilnerton High School, Pretoria, one of his history students was Dikgang Moseneke, who arrived on the island at the age of 15. Moseneke wanted to pursue an LLB and needed a pass in Latin:

On the island, Uncle Stan saw me through my first encounter with Latin grammar. Whilst the two of us were going about our mindless prison chores, such as pushing wheelbarrows, he would insist that I volubly rehearse Latin declensions and conjugations. As I went 'amo …, amas…, amat …', the prison warder would turn towards me, shake his head, convinced that I had lost it … I passed university Latin and later the LLB degree. (Moseneke, quoted in Mogoba 2004:iii)

There were political divisions on the island. But those who taught made it clear that their classes were for everybody. John Nyati Pokela, the PAC leader, was insistent: 'I'm a teacher by profession. I taught. I'm not going to teach only PAC people here. Anyone who wants education come!' (SADET 2008:290). Andrew Masondo, the MK cadre and mathematics lecturer, makes a similar point: 'As far as education was concerned, the fact that you belonged to a different political organization was immaterial to us. We taught anybody who needed to be taught, and anybody who could teach taught anybody' (SADET 2008:259).

Pencils and paper

In a population of ten thousand criminals, a couple of thousand politicals, hundreds of warders and guards, no one knows where the pen is – only the beetle and the little lizard and the boy who feeds them … What would the jailer do if he *found* the pen? Beat the boy to pulp? … As he held the pen in his fingers he imagined letting it go, dropping it into the stink … He gripped the pen tight in his hand and clicked the nib in and out … it said, a sound so fine, so mysterious – like the whisper of many words hidden in the ink – that he knew he could not do it. (Connelly 2008:231)

There was a dearth of material to write on and pencils and pens had to be strictly accounted for. It led to the most ingenious schemes to replenish resources.

As Sedick Isaacs explains, the prisoners found ways of using whatever materials they literally could lay their hands on:

Material to write on was one of the major problems confronting the prisoners. Pencils were cut into quarters and shared. And the other thing was slates. We bought slates because you could write on these slates and wipe it off. It was cheap once the initial cost was covered. Then, in the quarry, we broke slates and sometimes a nice big piece could also be used as a type of a slate. But slates were thus the means by which we could economise … because pencils were in short supply,

6

a pencil had to be cut into four segments and distributed. When I first went to solitary confinement, I had a short pencil. That is when I wrote my first textbook of mathematics on toilet paper.

Monde Mkunqwana recalls:

We would bring in the cement pockets, and those cement pockets would be transformed into exercise books and then pencils or ballpoint pens – they would be secured from the spans that were working in the married quarters or single quarters, or from the warders.

Johnson Mlambo, who spent 20 years on the island for PAC activities, remembers how they cut up the inside sheets of cement bags

nicely into small booklets and people would be able to write A, E, I, O, U, SA, SE, SI, SO, SU … the predominant section of the population came from migrant and peasant people. Many of them learnt reading and writing on the island against the organized might of the racist regime, which didn't want us to have any of that. (SADET 2008:291)

In the single cells Eddie Daniels remembers one of his favourite materials to write on 'was Sunlight soap wrappers, which were large compared to the wrappers of other items' (Daniels 1998:157).

The privilege of studying on paper stood in contrast to the fact that prisoners 'were not allowed to engage in creative writing – poetry or fiction … our cells were continually raided, our books ransacked for unauthorized scraps of writing' (Dingake 1987:181). Confiscation was a persistent theme. Kwedi Mkalipi, a member of the PAC who arrived on the island in 1966 to begin a 20-year sentence, speaks about how the authorities 'found a piece of paper in my pocket – a Reader's Digest article about Hiroshima. I was charged with possession of an unauthorized article' (Mkalipi, quoted in Schadeberg 1994:49). The usual punishment for this was to be 'put on a spare diet; for three days you get the juice of the mealie rice; on the fourth day you'd be given cooked mealies and the following three days the mealie rice liquid again; after that you would get half rations for a further 14 days' (Mkalipi, quoted in Schadeberg 1994:49).

University of South Africa

We certify that

EDWARD JOSEPH DANIELS

having complied with the requirements of the Act and Statute, was admitted to the degree of

Bachelor of Arts

at a congregation of the University

on 1 May 1976

Ivanhijk
Vice-Chancellor

A. S. Roux.
Dean

MHStockhoff
Registrar

PRETORIA

The Bachelor of Arts degree obtained by Eddie Daniels in prison.

One of the two degrees Eddie Daniels received on the island.

Without study privilege many of the prisoners would have atrophied intellectually and bouts of demoralisation might have superseded the general buoyancy of the community. Studies to a large extent played some diversionary role. It is true the majority of prisoners did not enjoy the formal privilege of study while they were in gaol for a number of reasons, the principal one being lack of funds. Informally, no prisoner who had an interest in learning failed to benefit from the intellectual atmosphere that prevailed. The privileged students took risks, 'abused' their study privilege to help their less privileged fellow inmates. (Dingake 1987:183–184).[2]

Echoing Dingake's concerns, Natoo Babenia, who spent 16 years on Robben Island warned, 'if you do not watch out prison can put your brain to death' (1995:167), what Mac Maharaj called 'a state of mental ennui' could overwhelm one (quoted in Buntman 2003:78). In the prison context it became important to 'discipline yourself intellectually by stealing with ears and with eyes, attempting in all possible ways to feed the mind' (Breytenbach 1984:255–256). Zwelonke writes of how in the general cells in the 1960s when they were cut off from what was going on in the outside world, they learnt to read the expressions of the warders:

Widening wrinkles in fits of anger, or smiles of triumph; red, glaring eyes and louder mouths when faced with setbacks, or drawling self-flattery when they were happy about something. So went our news commentary. But not all the warders knew anything about the shifting sands of world politics. It was the top warders who read newspapers and passed on their moods to the juniors. Receiving such news at second-hand, in a distorted form, these warders became either angry hyenas or circus clowns. (Zwelonke 1989:65)

Sometimes the quest 'to feed the mind' meant literally stealing. 'On one occasion a Brother September was the visiting cleric for the Sunday service. During the service, Hennie Ferris and Eddie Daniels stole a newspaper from the Brother's satchel while he was earnestly praying' (Sisulu 2004:294). But it was not just to read, but to read 'against the grain' (Benjamin 1968:257). Prisoners were allowed a number of magazines that were government propaganda. 'Political prisoners read them "critically" by simply standing "the news on its head", so that if an

article in a government journal argued that Bantu Education was being accepted, they concluded that it was in fact being resisted. They learned much by reading this way' (Dick 2007:37).

A great deal of effort and time was spent transcribing books in order to distribute literature among the cells. As Sedick Isaacs remembers:

I studied book writing, before the printing press. In monasteries ... monks used to sit and rewrite books for publication. In the night when it is cold, and then you would see prisoners sit wrapped in a blanket with a pen, writing out the books. I thought this really looked like a monastery. Of course there were people who tried to illustrate their books also. By illustrate I mean a fancy type of lettering. They were writing the text book for themselves, and then the copied 'text book' was later passed on to other people.

Reading movies

We were intrigued by *The King and I*, for to us it depicted the clash between the values of East and West, and seemed to suggest that the West had much to learn from the East. Cleopatra proved controversial; many of my comrades took exception to the fact that the queen of Egypt was depicted by a raven-haired, violet-eyed American actress, however beautiful. The detractors asserted that the movie was an example of Western propaganda that sought to erase the fact that Cleopatra was an African woman. (Mandela 1994:488)

The islanders were not only reading books but also reading movies. Around the mid-1970s, inmates were allowed to watch movies. Sedick Isaacs explains how the warders and prisoners sometimes shared the films:

There was a Warders' Film Club, and we would negotiate that to be also shown to us as well. Whatever the warders hired for that weekend was then also shown to us on Saturday. They first wanted us to contribute, but we resisted that. I said, 'Well, it is there. Then, in any case, you might as well let us see the movies. You can't take it back. It is no extra cost.' I think Willemse – he was one of the commanding officers – finally agreed with that and said, 'Show it to them.'

There was also a committee which vetted the films to be shown to prisoners. Isaacs recalls:

> We saw films like *The Green Beret*. But one week they brought a film and the Head of Prison came to announce to us that the film we had this week had been considered 'not suitable for prisoners' and, on that occasion it was censored. I was on the negotiating committee at that time. I went to the second in charge, the chief warder. I said, 'What is the film?' He said, 'It's *The Ten Commandments*.' I couldn't believe that. I thought he was joking. I asked what is wrong with *The Ten Commandments* and he said, 'It shows a bit of resistance' ... It must be a part where the Israelites revolt against the Pharaoh. What the head of the prison saw as *opstokery* (instigation). That is why *The Ten Commandments* was banned for prisoners.

After a while, prisoners were also allowed documentaries. When a documentary on Hell's Angels was shown, the discussion that followed was overwhelmingly met with criticism of the

> Hell's Angels for their lawless ways. But then Strini Moodley, a bright young Black Consciousness member, stood up and accused the assembled group of being out of touch with the times, for they represented the equivalent of the Soweto students of 1976 who rebelled against the authorities. He reproached us for being elderly, middle class intellectuals who identified with the movie's right-wing authorities instead of the bikers. (Mandela 1994:489)

As Moodley remembers, he cautioned that they

> should look at the symbolism of the movie ... the film condoned institutionalized violence, but condemned anti-system violence. There was a furore against me. I was accused of supporting a bunch of rapists and of downright unmitigated evil. My talk of symbolism, I was told was just so much hogwash. (Meer 1988:274)

Mandela asked Moodley to prepare a paper on the subject. 'I prepared the paper and there was great interest and unemotional intellectual discussion' (Meer 1988:274).

It was not as if the prisoners were only watching the movies and documentaries with critical intensity. Mandela writes of how 'films were a wonderful diversion' and when they 'saw local South African films with black stars ... our little makeshift theatre echoed with the shouts, whistles and cheers that greeted an old friend on screen' (Mandela 1994:488). Ahmed Kathrada, who was the single section's librarian, was aware of not falling 'into the groove of seeking a social message in every film, novel, cartoon or comic', highlighting this through a wonderful story:

> [O]n days when the 1956–61 Treason Trial became very boring some of us devised alternative forms of entertainment. We used to bring along cartoon books ('Andy Capp', 'Bringing up Father', etc) and enjoy ourselves. One day my neighbor and I decided to circulate Andy Capp among all the accused, and observe the various reactions. Some obviously enjoyed it; others were indifferent; some simply could not fathom what was going on. A few hours later I received a note: 'Comrade', it said, 'What has all this to do with Marxism-Leninism?'!! (Quoted in Vahed & Waetjen 2009:203)

The past and the present

> If you ever go visiting in Capetown
>
> and look across that blue and silver bay
>
> spare a thought for those who ploughed
>
> the gray miles of water
>
> salt and bitter as their tears
>
> who stir in graves as restless as the surge
>
> and wonder if they gave their lives in vain.
>
> — Dennis Brutus, 1996

What then of the present? Are the new political leaders upholding the traditions that were so central to the struggle to defeat apartheid and

9

build a new South Africa? Hein Marais' work presents a sobering snapshot of the state of schooling in South Africa:

> In multi-country surveys, the numeracy and literacy levels of young South Africans lag behind those of many other African countries. In the 40-country *Progress in International Reading Literacy Study* carried out in 2006, South Africa was the worst performer. According to a Department of Education national study of Grade Six learners, only 19% of learners could do mathematics and only 37% could read and write in the language of instruction, at the appropriate grade level. Among the problems listed in the report were school fees and access to information (at school), school libraries, textbooks and learning materials. (Marais 2011:323)

In 2008, Neville Alexander was among the educationists who highlighted the state of school education in an open letter:

> Too many schools are unsafe, bleak, uninspiring places where violence and abuse are rife. Teachers and their students are too often traumatized, demotivated and merely going through the motions. Schools as learning spaces, where opportunities exist for experiencing the joy of learning, exploring, experimenting and achieving, are few and far between. When they do exist they are to be found mainly in established suburban, former white areas. (Alexander et al 2008, quoted in Marais 2011:328)

In 2011, 17 years after the first democratic elections, only between 2% and 8% of schools in South Africa have libraries, while in 2010, a huge chunk of the budget for libraries was unused (*The Mercury* 17 February 2011; *The Mercury* 29 March 2011).

Remembering the stories of such passion for learning on Robben Island must be seen not only as an act of historical memory but also as a critical examination of the past as a means of responding to challenges in the present. Not to be imprisoned by history but to make it.

WILLIAM
SHAKESPEARE

THE COMPLETE WORKS

A new edition, edited with an
introduction and glossary by
PETER ALEXANDER
*Professor Emeritus of English Language and
Literature, University of Glasgow*

COLLINS
LONDON AND GLASGOW

Prison number: 183/72. Sonny Venkatrathnam, a
member of the African People's Democratic Union of
Southern Africa, used postcards sent by his family to
cover his copy of William Shakespeare's *The Complete
Works*. In these pages former Robben Island political
prisoners signed off on sections that appealed to
them, or sections that moved them.

SONNY VENKATRATHNAM

Between the 'Bible' and the Bard

> ... Remember
>
> First to possess his books
>
> *The Tempest*, Act III, Scene 2

The inmates of Robben Island hungered after books that could both engage and stimulate them over prolonged periods. There was much anticipation when Sonny Venkatrathnam,[3] a member of the African People's Democratic Union of Southern Africa (Apdusa) incarcerated on Robben Island in the 1970s, received a copy of *The Complete Works of Shakespeare*.[4] But it was soon confiscated. He was shattered but always kept a hope that he would gain access once more to his beloved Shakespeare. And then the atheist was saved by divine intervention:

> And one Sunday morning, I remember ... a warder ... tells me, 'The church is here.' I said, 'Church, what church?' He says, 'The Anglican Church.' You see, it was a practice every Sunday; either the Methodist or the Roman Catholics or Dutch Reformed or whoever, comes ... holds services in the section ... I tell him I'm an Anglican you know but I left my Bible in the storeroom. Okay, he says, he'll open the storeroom. He takes out his keys; opens the storeroom; and I pick out

> my book: *The Complete Works of Shakespeare*. I take it out and show it to him, 'look there's the Bible by William Shakespeare'. So he let me have it, I took it to my cell and we were celebrating ... The problem is how we hide it because there is nothing ... it's a bare room, you see, we didn't even have cupboards, nothing ...

> So what I did was that, again providentially, it was Deepavali, and my parents sent me greeting cards. These are your typical Deepavali greeting cards. So I took those cards, cut them up and pasted the photographs on this [book] and we used porridge to stick it up. It's the way it is since I had it on Robben Island. And I openly left this on the window sill, right behind my bed. They would come and ask me, 'What's that?' And I said, 'It's my Bible.' The ... Afrikaner, there are two things he's scared of: his God and his Bible, and a lawyer ... So I had this, they did not touch it.

If ever there was a case of not judging a book by its cover, then it was Venkatrathnam's *The Complete Works of Shakespeare*. Victor Hugo, author of *Les Misérables*, wrote that 'England has two books, the Bible and Shakespeare'. On another island, ten thousand kilometres away, the two mutated into one.

There was a camaraderie on the island, political discussions amid the struggle to survive. For Venkatrathnam, there was Shakespeare. As time stood still on the island and the isolation and longing conspired to overwhelm him, Venkatrathnam turned to Shakespeare to transport him to another world, 'a world that can bring you happiness … particularly in times of sadness' (Pamuk 2007:110).

Venkatrathnam's interest in Shakespeare was sparked by an extended essay he wrote in his final year at the University of Natal that focused on Shakespeare's jesters. On a trip to Stratford-upon-Avon in 2006, Elizabeth Woledge for the publication, *Shakespeare at the Centre*, asked Venkatrathnam 'whether the prisoners had enjoyed the lighter moments which Shakespeare created, or only the stirring political commentary'. Venkatrathnam responded: 'The comic relief? The jesters and fools? Yes we did enjoy them … the fools are the philosophers of Shakespeare. I don't think I saw it as light because I saw it as the philosophy of Shakespeare coming out' (Woledge 2006:11).

For people such as Venkatrathnam, Shakespeare was not simply about bringing some solace in a brutal environment. Shakespeare could be read in ways that spoke to the political context of the times or as Rob Nixon puts it, as 'responsive to indigenous interests and needs' (1987:229), contesting the traditional Eurocentric ways in which Shakespeare was read.

As Venkatrathnam prepared to leave Robben Island, he sent his treasured *Shakespeare* around to his fellow single cell comrades and asked each one to choose a line or a paragraph that spoke to them.

Selections from prison

The prison setting suddenly made so many lines resonate with new meaning. Sonny told me about the night he'd heard a voice echoing down the corridor of cells, crying out: 'What a piece of work is a man …' 'Which section did you sign?' I asked Sonny. He grinned – 'All of it!' – and turned the book on its side: written across the thick slab of pages were his initials. 'And which would you have signed?' he asked. I answered without hesitation: 'Tomorrow and tomorrow and tomorrow.' When I played Macbeth in 1999, that speech never ceased

THE 'ROBBEN ISLAND' SHAKESPEARE

Sonny Venkatrathnam's copy of Shakespeare was circulated amongst leading African nationalist prisoners on Robben Island, who autographed and dated their favourite passages.

The book is open to show the lines marked, and signed, by Nelson Mandela. They are spoken by Julius Caesar in answer to his wife Calpurnia, who has begged him not to go to the Senate House.

'Cowards die many times before their deaths;
The valiant never taste of death but once.
Of all the wonders that I yet have heard,
It seems to me most strange that men should fear,
Seeing that death, a necessary end,
Will come when it will come.'

Sonny Venkatrathnam's *Shakespeare* on display at Stratford-upon-Avon.

LENNOX,

's are near at

ot it nothing.
fore us?
d of Birnam.
him down a

reby shall we
5
nd make dis-

lone.
t the confident

nd will endure

nain hope; 10
ge to be given,

To hear a night-shriek
hair
Would at a dismal treatise rouse and stir
As life were in't. I have supp'd full with
horrors;
Direness, familiar to my slaughterous
thoughts,
Cannot once start me.

Re-enter SEYTON.

Wherefore was that cry? 15
Sey. The Queen, my lord, is dead.
Macb. She should have died hereafter;
There would have been a time for such a
word.
To-morrow, and to-morrow, and to-morrow,
Creeps in this petty pace from day to day
To the last syllable of recorded time, 21
And all our yesterdays have lighted fools
The way to dusty death. Out, out, brief
candle!
Life's but a walking shadow, a poor player,

E. J. Daniels.

Liberal Party member Eddie Daniels signed off on *Macbeth*.

to send a chill up my spine. Sonny and I looked it up, and sure enough, prisoner E. J. Daniels had signed it. (Antony Sher)[5]

Eddie Daniels arrived on the island in November 1964 to serve a 15-year sentence. The beginnings were tough:

> My isolation cell was like a death chamber, totally silent and everything around me was grey, cold, bleak and frightening. At first I could not eat the prison food because it stank, but after two weeks I started to eat just to survive. (Quoted in Schadeberg 1994:53)

But Daniels soon found camaraderie and deep friendships that eased the suffering and sense of isolation. This was important as he was the only

member of the Liberal Party on the island. His fellow accused from the Liberal Party and its offshoot, the African Resistance Movement (ARM), were all white and incarcerated in other prisons. This isolation from his comrades was exacerbated by the fact that his friend and fellow ARM member, Adrian Leftwich, had given damaging evidence against him (Lewin 2011:85).[6]

Daniels had joined the Liberal Party after attending one of its meetings on Cape Town's Grand Parade. He joined because 'it satisfied the criteria that I was seeking, both being anti-government and non-racial' (Daniels 1998:93).

As indicated by Antony Sher, he chose a piece from *Macbeth*. Unlike many of the other prisoners in the single cell section, Daniels had no secondary school education. Growing up in poverty in District Six and then Lavender Hill, he worked in a shoe factory, a printing works and then on a trawler. For Eddie Daniels,[7]

> Shakespeare was a voyage of discovery. I never knew about Shakespeare, never heard of Shakespeare at primary school, but when I discovered Shakespeare, it was beautiful, it was beautiful you know. It was a voyage of discovery for me. And I took part in a play, we were allowed about five plays before the prison authorities stopped it. I was Mark Anthony ... to read, you know ... to read books which I never ever dreamt of reading was beautiful.

While one should not read too much into what prisoners chose, some of the selections give rare insights into their personalities and their desires. The fact that many took the request seriously and made choices that spoke beyond the confines of the island makes the selections even more poignant (Hofmeyr 2006 provides a fascinating account of why ANC leaders had a penchant for quoting Shakespeare).

Julius Caesar

Nelson Mandela chose the words of *Julius Caesar* drawn from Caesar's reaction to the pleadings of his wife, Calpurnia, not to go to the Senate:

CAESAR:

Cowards die many times before their deaths:

The valiant never taste of death but once.

Of all the wonders that I yet have heard,

It seems to be most strange that men should fear;

Seeing that death, a necessary end,

Will come, when it will come.

Act II, Scene 2

When Mandela signed off on *Julius Caesar*, it must have taken him back to three decades earlier to 1944, when he was part of drawing up the manifesto for the Youth League of the African National Congress and penned the following words:

CASSIUS:

The fault, dear Brutus, is not in our stars … But in
ourselves, that we are underlings.

Act I, Scene 3

In the 1950s in Mandela's Johannesburg, Shakespeare was leaned on by the writers of *Drum,* most notably Can Themba, in relating to the conditions of apartheid South Africa (Johnson 1996; Distiller 2005). Bloke Modisane, in his autobiography first published in 1963, makes constant reference to Shakespeare to illustrate life in Sophiatown; the dilemmas of the quest for freedom and the use of violence:

> My sensibilities have been dulled by the violence of oppression, my energy has been dissipated by the struggles, the plots, the repressed violence simmering within my body, the insatiate demand for the blood of the oppressors; I had reasoned myself that only in blood will I see an end to my oppression or be myself destroyed. This was the harsh reality. It had been impressed on me that only in the blood of Caesar could the conspirators prevent the abuse of power

> which might sway Caesar more than his reason; but it was Brutus who realised the margin between power and physical man, warning that since the 'quarrel will bear no colour to the thing he is', let us concern ourselves with the destruction of a symbol, which we hate, but not the man. Like Brutus, I am haunted by the immediacy, the direct presence of blood between oppression and the freedom which I must snatch. (Modisane 1986:230–231)

Two decades later, facing the death penalty, Mandela recalls drawing on these haunting words from *Measure for Measure* (Mandela 1994:360):

Be absolute for death; either death or life

Shall thereby be the sweeter.

Act III, Scene 1

Shakespeare followed Mandela. At his 80th birthday in 1998, Thabo Mbeki spoke these words from *King Lear*:

… and tell old tales, and laugh

At gilded butterflies, and hear poor rogues

Talk of court news.

Act V, Scene 3

Was this an appropriate selection? These words to a man who had spent so much of his life cut off from the world and his family? In the event, Mbeki's hope that Mandela's influence would decline and he would get on with the serious business of governance and transformation was premature. Mandela still held court after his retirement in 1999, much to the frustration of Mbeki who reputedly after a time did not take Mandela's calls or return them (Sampson 2008). As if out of the Shakespearean handbook, it is Mbeki who is forced to renounce power and have those who most flattered him, the Regans and Gonerils, abandon him for the new wielders of power.

Shakespeare is a persistent theme in Mandela's life. But this English influence went further and was central to Mandela's outlook. Anthony Sampson, author of Mandela's official biography, writes of Mandela's visit to Britain:

> I watched him entertaining the Queen at a banquet, arguing with academics at Oxford, jiving at Albert Hall, embracing children in London streets … He loved talking about his English education and influences, and he often sounded less like an African president or chief than a Victorian gentleman, maintaining old-fashioned attitudes that the British had lost. He would quote from Tennyson's 'In Memoriam', from Wordsworth or from W. E. Henley: 'I am master of my fate' … Like other colonial subjects, including his own mentor, Jawaharlal Nehru, he seemed to have absorbed English ideals of fairness and morality more thoroughly than the English themselves. (Sampson 2008:249)

Some would argue that Mandela was symptomatic of Fanon's black middle class who 'remembers what it has read in European textbooks and imperceptibly it becomes not even the replica of Europe, but its caricature' (Fanon 1967:141). Or was this a tactical response? Mandela the thespian, putting on another performance? It was not as if Mandela was unaware of the tensions. While he possessed a copy of *The Oxford Book of English Verse* on Robben Island, he hankered after Xhosa poets, 'who gave expression to my own aspirations and dreams, who flatter my national pride, and who give me a sense of destiny and achievement' and felt the need to assert that 'Western culture has not entirely rubbed off my African background' (Sampson 1999:286). It is frequently forgotten that national liberation movements were 'often led by lawyers, doctors, and writers who were partly formed and to some degree produced by the colonial power' (Said 1994:269).

Anthony Sampson, who had unprecedented access to Mandela, provides a clue to how difficult it is to *read* him:

Nelson Mandela's signature in Sonny Venkatrathnam's *Shakespeare*.

JULIUS CÆSAR

Fierce fiery warriors fight upon the clouds,
In ranks and squadrons and right form of war, 20
Which drizzled blood upon the Capitol ;
The noise of battle hurtled in the air ;
Horses did neigh, and dying men did groan,
And ghosts did shriek and squeal about the streets.
O Cæsar, these things are beyond all use, 25
And I do fear them !
    Cæs.   What can be avoided,
Whose end is purpos'd by the mighty gods ?
Yet Cæsar shall go forth ; for these predictions
Are to the world in general as to Cæsar.
    Cal. When beggars die there are no comets seen : 30
The heavens themselves blaze forth the death of princes.
    Cæs. Cowards die many times before their deaths :
The valiant never taste of death but once.
Of all the wonders that I yet have heard,
It seems to me most strange that men should fear, 35
Seeing that death, a necessary end,
Will come when it will come.

            Re-enter Servant.

                    What say the augurers ?
    Serv. They would not have you to stir forth to-day.
Plucking the entrails of an offering forth,
They could not find a heart within the beast. 40
    Cæs. The gods do this in shame of cowardice.
Cæsar should be a beast without a heart,
If he should stay at home to-day for fear.
No, Cæsar shall not. Danger knows full well
That Cæsar is more dangerous than he : 45
We are two lions litter'd in one day,
And I the elder and more terrible ;
And Cæsar shall go forth.
    Cal.   Alas, my lord,
Your wisdom is consum'd in confidence.
Do not go forth to-day. Call it my fear 50
That keeps you in the house, and not your own.
We'll send Mark Antony to the Senate House,
And he shall say you are not well to-day.
Let me, upon my knee, prevail in this.
    Cæs. Mark Antony shall say I am not well ; 55
And for thy humour I will stay at home.

            Enter DECIUS.

Here's Decius Brutus, he shall tell them so.
    Dec. Cæsar, all hail ! Good morrow, worthy Cæsar.
I come to fetch you to the Senate House.
    Cæs. And you are come in very happy time, 60

980

To bear my gr
And tell them
Cannot, is fa
            falser
I will not co
            Decius
Cal. Say he
Cæs.
Have I in co
            so far,
To be afeard t
Decius, go tell
    Dec. Most u
            some o
Lest I be laugh
    Cæs. The ca
            come.
That is enough
But for your p
Because I love
Calphurnia he
            home.
She dreamt to
Which, like a
            spouts
Did run pure
            Roma
Came smiling
            in it.
And these doe
            porte
And evils imm
Hath begg'd t
            day.
    Dec. This d
It was a vision
Your statue sp
In which so m
Signifies that
            suck
Reviving bloo
            press
For tinctures,
This by Calph
    Cæs. And
            pound
    Dec. I have
            I can
And know it
            cludes
To give this o
If you shall s
            come,
Their minds
            a mo
Apt to be rer
' Break up th
When Cæsar'
            dream
If Cæsar hi
            whisp
' Lo, Cæsar is
Pardon me, C
To your proc

I could still not penetrate behind the hearty and amiable style of the man who was so near and yet so far. He was always the politician, who had merged his public personality with his private feelings everywhere except in his home. Richard Stengel, who ghosted his autobiography, had forewarned me: 'The man and the mask are one,' and Ahmed Kathrada, who had been with him in prison for twenty-five years, had admitted: 'He's impenetrable.' (Sampson 2008:251)

In Sampson's biography of Mandela, chapter 28 is titled 'Man and Myth'. If it is difficult to read Mandela, it is as difficult to *write* Mandela, as man and myth have converged. How like Caesar. As Maslen and Schmidt point out, over time it has become hard to distinguish Caesar with his 'weaknesses: his deafness, his epileptic fits, his overbearing arrogance' from the 'myth of Caesar that has endured throughout the centuries'. The power of the myth 'is confirmed by the fact that Emperors have donned Caesar's surname like a robe of office ever since' (Maslen & Schmidt 2008:103).

One of Sonny Venkatrathnam's drawings made on Robben Island.

Andrew Masondo had an honours degree in applied mathematics from Wits University and began lecturing at the age of 24 at the University of Fort Hare. Masondo grew up in Johannesburg, moving between Sophiatown, White City, Jabavu and Alexandra through the 1940s and first decade of the 1950s. For Lewis Nkosi, a time when:

> It was the cacophonous, swaggering world of Elizabethan England which gave us the closest parallel to our own mode of existence; the cloak and dagger stories of Shakespeare; the marvellously gay and dangerous time of change in Great Britain came close to reflecting our own condition. Thus it was possible for an African musician returning home at night to inspire awe in a group of thugs surrounding him by declaiming in an impossibly archaic English: 'Unhand me, rogues!' Indeed, they did unhand him. The same thugs who were to be seen chewing on apples in the streets of Johannesburg after the picture *Street with no Name*, also delighted in the violent colour, the rolling rhetoric of Shakespearean theatre. Their favourite form of persecuting middle-class Africans was forcing them to stand at street corners, reciting some passage from Shakespeare, for which they would be showered with sincere applause. (Nkosi 1983:13)

Involved in Umkhonto we Sizwe (MK) activities at Fort Hare, Masondo's unit was hobbled by a lack of equipment. His unit took to sawing off wooden pylons in what he called 'cold demolition'. The unit was arrested and Masondo was sentenced to 12 years on the island.

Shocked by the fact that there were prisoners who could not read or write, Masondo got involved in literacy classes. Without any stationery they made books out of cement bags.

> We asked our common law comrades, because they worked in offices, to get us pencils and things of that nature and smuggle them into our cells ... Nothing to read! So we would write out these little books, little stories and sentences, to teach these other people. (Masondo, quoted in SADET 2008:259)

Beyond the literacy classes, Masondo taught Matric level maths, Xhosa, Zulu, and Tswana as well as degree level applied mathematics. 'The best times of my teaching were on Robben Island. In fact, in my whole life, the greatest and most satisfying teaching that I ever did was on the island' (SADET 2008:259).

He also chose from *Julius Caesar*:

ANTONY:

Oh, pardon me, thou bleeding piece of earth,

That I am meek and gentle with these butchers!

Thou art the ruins of the noblest man

That ever lived in the tide of times.

Woe to the hand that shed this costly blood!

Over thy wounds now do I prophesy, —

Which, like dumb mouths, do ope their ruby lips,

To beg the voice and utterance of my tongue —

Act III, Scene 1

Reflecting on Masondo's choice, Venkatrathnam wryly comments that Masondo was to go on to be one of the enforcers at Quatro, the notorious ANC camp in Angola (Trewhela 2009). In post-apartheid South Africa, he served in the South African National Defence Force (SANDF). But Masondo's choice also probably reflects the brutality that he personally faced at the hands of the warders on the island.

Dennis Brutus bears witness:

> [T]he prisoners who were brought in were called the Masondo group, after Andrew Masondo … What had happened was that the guards had consistently ill-treated Masondo, in the place where he was working with his squad. Masondo had protested this, and as punishment he had been tied to a stake in the centre of his working group, and denied the opportunity to go to the toilet or to drink water. And he had been left there for some time, in the sun … So they were being marched in to be disciplined. They were lined up, with rows of guards facing them; the guards were armed with batons, or leather straps, and their report was made to a young slim officer called Lt Frazer, who, after hearing the complaint, had issued a command in a quiet, almost conversational voice and had said, 'Carry on' … When the instruction is given to 'carry on' it means the guards are free to do pretty much anything to the prisoners. In this instance they waded in to the prisoners with batons and straps and sticks and then grabbed wooden pick handles and staves from a nearby storing shed … It was an indescribable fury unleashed. (Sustar & Karim 2006:74–75)

King Lear

As the ANC regrouped in exile, it entered into an alliance with Joshua Nkomo's Zimbabwean African People's Union (Zapu). Joint operations took place against Rhodesian forces at the end of 1967 that came to be known as the Wankie Campaign. After the turn to the armed struggle in the early 1960s, these were the second generation of MK fighters. One of the leaders of the Luthuli Brigade involved in the fighting was Justice Mpanza. He was captured and sentenced to life imprisonment. *King Lear* was his choice, choosing the words of Edgar:

EDGAR:

The weight of this sad time we must obey;

Speak what we feel, not what we ought to say.

The oldest hath borne most: we that are young

Shall never see so much, nor live so long.

Act V, Scene 3

J. B. Vusani, a lawyer and member of Apdusa, spent a lot of his energy teaching those who could not read the basic alphabet. To this end he would smuggle a slate from the quarries, write a single alphabet and get prisoners to copy it. Vusani would also read to prisoners in Xhosa from *King Lear*. Many were peasants from rural Transkei.

These peasants had rebelled as they were dispossessed of their land, many put on the move to barren reserves or forced into the most soul destroying of labour on the mines. They listened in silence as Vusani spoke Gloucester's words at the end of a brutal day's labour in the quarry:

> So distribution should
> undo excess
>
> And each man have
> enough

Act IV, Scene 1

And whistles in ...
That ends this strange eventful history,
Is second childishness and mere oblivion;
Sans teeth, sans eyes, sans taste, sans every
    thing.   166

Re-enter ORLANDO *with* ADAM.

Duke S. Welcome.   Set down your
    venerable burden.
And let him feed.
Orl. I thank you most for him.
Adam.   So had you need;
I scarce can speak to thank you for myself.
Duke S. Welcome; fall to. I will not
    trouble you   171
As yet to question you about your fortunes.
Give us some music; and, good cousin,
    sing.

266

J B Vusani
2:1:78

Find out ...
Seek him with candle; bring hi
    living
Within this twelvemonth, or tu
    more
To seek a living in our territory.
Thy lands and all things that tho
    thine
Worth seizure do we seize into
Till thou canst quit thee by thy
    mouth
Of what we think against thee.
    Oli. O that your Highness kne
    in this!
I never lov'd my brother in my
    Duke F. More villain thou.
    him out of doors;

Venkatrathnam remembers that the prisoners would get agitated when Vusani read sections about Lear in power and would blurt out, 'What's wrong with the stupid King, why did he not get the elders to advise him?' Venkatrathnam also speaks about the connection the prisoners made in *King Lear*, from those with an 'English'-influenced university education to peasants from the Transkei: 'the way Shakespeare treats Lear's daughters; that of a typical universality, the favouring of one child above the other!' that was the suture (Woledge 2006:11).

Venkatrathnam's favourite Shakespeare is *King Lear*: 'It is so universal; the frailty of human nature, weaknesses, strengths, they have come out so well in King Lear and they are almost replicated by families you know' (Woledge 2006:11).

But when Vusani had to choose, it was not from *King Lear*, but from what is often described as the comedies of Shakespeare.

J B Vusani, a member of the African People's Democratic Union of Southern Africa, signed off on Shakespeare's *As You Like It* in Venkatrathnam's copy.

The comedies

> All the world's a stage,
>
> And all the men and women mere players:
>
> They have their exits and their entrances

Act II, Scene 7

Vusani's choice of the above lines from *As You Like It* at one level could be seen as a strange selection for someone who lived his life in the belief that history could be changed by political action. But it points to a deeper understanding. People have to play different roles in their lives and Vusani, the lawyer who hailed from the Transkei as Venkatrathnam surmises was using both his knowledge of traditions, together with his own university training to teach people who had no access to the written word. *As You Like It* speaks to the brutal use of power but also evokes the world of Duke Senior cast out to live in a forest. Here, in trying to create a just society where people are free to speak their minds, traditions of the past are not forgotten: 'The constant service of the antique world/When service sweat for duty, not for meed.' This was where Vusani stood, aware of a world that the peasants knew to be slowly but inexorably crushed, as the alienation of the land made 'it unlawful for black men to keep milk cows of their own' and made 'many poor people homeless' (Plaatje, quoted in Orkin 1987:164) and the stark contrasting world of law books and Shakespeare.

It stirs the imagination to think of Vusani sitting in a cell on Robben Island reading *King Lear* to those dispossessed of their land and sitting in rags:

Poor naked wretches, whereso'er you are,

That bide the pelting of this pitiless storm,

How shall your houseless heads and unfed sides,

Your loop'd and window'd raggedness, defend you

From seasons such as these?

Act III, Scene 4

Mobbs Gqirana, a long-term PAC inmate disappeared after his release. Venkatrathnam believes he was murdered by the apartheid regime. Given the quest to educate themselves while doing hard labour in the quarries, listening and passing on knowledge to others, Gqirana's choice from *As You Like It* is pointed:

Sweet are the uses of adversity;

Which, like the toad, ugly and venomous,

Wears yet a precious jewel in his head;

And this our life, exempt from public haunt,

Finds tongues in trees, books in the running brooks,

Sermons in stones, and good in everything.

Act II, Scene 1

Kwedi Mkalipi,[8] serving a 20-year sentence, chose from *A Midsummer Night's Dream*:

So shall all couples three.

Ever true in loving be.

Act V, Scene 1

For Mkalipi, *A Midsummer Night's Dream* gave him inspiration in the dark days when he missed his wife and family. It spoke to him that love will prevail.

Kwedi Mkalipi, a member of the Pan-Africanist Congress of Azania, chose a passage from *Midsummer Night's Dream* in Venkatrathnam's copy of *Shakespeare*.

21

As we sit in the Mowbray offices of Azanian People's Liberation Army (Apla) veterans surrounded by ageing PAC members, many of whom spent decades of their lives on the island, Mkalipi says his favourite Shakespeare line on the island was from Lady Macbeth: 'All the perfumes of Arabia will not sweeten this little hand.' For him, the attempts of apartheid's rulers to sweeten the outer edifice through Bantustans and the promise of early release if the veterans renounced violence were not enough. For Mkalipi, the whole of apartheid had to go and it was this that sustained him.

Andrew Mlangeni, member of MK High Command and Rivonia triallist, chose to re-read Lady Macbeth's wanton pledge to violence into the commitment to destroy apartheid. Fadiman's reminder that 'a book belongs to the reader as well as the writer' is apposite (2007:89).

I have given suck, and know

How tender tis to love the babe that milks me –

I would, while it was smiling in my face,

Have pluck'd my nipple from his boneless gums,

And dash'd the brains out, had I so sworn

As you have done to this.

Macbeth, Act I, Scene 7

Unlike many of the other luminaries in the single cells, Govan Mbeki chose a passage from *Twelfth Night*:

If music be the food of love play on,

Give me excess of it ...

Act I, Scene 1

Music clearly was a love in his life. Mbeki talks about organising

concerts for birthdays or for the end of the year, and we would sit at the windows and sing songs or recite poems. A range of music came through those windows, including 'Blue River', ... 'Be Mine'. You would clap your hands and the sound would travel through the windows ... I had a guitar in prison ... I played the guitar quite a lot, at first with Neville Alexander and then with a group of other prisoners. (Mbeki, quoted in Schadeberg 1994:30)

Walter Sisulu, born of a Xhosa woman and a white man, chose hauntingly from the words of Shylock in the *Merchant of Venice*:

For suff'rance is the badge of all our tribe;

You call me misbeliever, cut-throat dog,

And spit upon my Jewish gaberdine.

The use of Shylock had a long lineage in the ANC, with one of its founding members, Sol Plaatje, evoking one of his oft quoted lines (quoted in Couzens & Willan 1976:7):

With apologies to Shakespeare's *Merchant of Venice*

Hath not a Mochuana eyes?

Hath he not hands, organs, dimensions, senses, affections, passions??

Is not a Mochuana fed with the same food, hurt with the same weapons, subject to the same diseases, healed by the same means, warmed and cooled by the same winter and summer, as a whiteman is??

If you prick us, do we not bleed? If you tickle us, do we not laugh? If you poison us, do we not die?

And if you wrong us shall we not revenge? If we are like you in the rest we will resemble you in that.

Sisulu was known for his patience and empathy to prisoners across the political spectrum. His refusal to be provoked was legendary. Ahmed Kathrada, who spent nearly three decades imprisoned with Sisulu, read

Antony's words from *Julius Caesar* to bid farewell to Walter Sisulu: 'His life was gentle; and the elements; so much mixed in him, that Nature might stand up, And say to all the world, "This was a Man!"'

Hamlet

> Hamlet doubts because he remembers. He acts because he remembers. Where others forget or wish to forget, Hamlet shoulders the burden of remembering and of reminding everyone of their obligation to be or not to be ... Macbeth on the other hand, wishes to forget, to render memory nothing more than 'fume' ... What a contrast with Hamlet and his fervent desire to maintain his memory ever 'green', like the everlasting plant of life. (Fuentes 238:2005)

Hamlet as the keeper of memory. Whose memory, whose legitimacy, whose tradition?

The new generation of Black Consciousness (BC) adherents arrived on the island in the mid 1970s. Mandela describes their arrival:

> These young men were a different breed of prisoner from those we had seen before. They were brave, hostile and aggressive; they would not take orders and shout '*Amandla*' at every opportunity. Their instinct was to confront rather than to cooperate. The authorities did not know how to handle them, and they turned the island upside down ... It was obvious that they regarded us, the Rivonia Triallists, as moderates. After so many years of being branded a radical revolutionary, to be perceived as a moderate was a novel and not altogether pleasant feeling. (Mandela 1994:471)

Both BC-aligned prisoners, Saths Cooper[9] and Strini Moodley, chose from *Hamlet*.

Cooper:

> HAMLET:
> This heavy-headed revel east and west
> Make us traduc'd and tax'd of other nations

They clepe us drunkards, and with swinish phrase
Soil our addition; and indeed, it takes
From our achievements, though perform'd at height
The pith and marrow of our attribute.
So, oft it chances in particular men
That, for somew vicious mole of nature in them,
Since nature cannot choose his origin;
By the o'ergrowth of some complexion,
Oft breaking down the pales and forts of reason;
Or by some habit that too much o'er leavens
The form of plausive manners – that these men,
Carrying, I say, the stamp of one defect
Being nature's livery or fortunes star,
His virtues else, be they as pure as grace
As infinite as man may undergo.
Shall in the general censure take corruption
From that particular fault. The dram of eale
Doth all the noble substance of a doubt
To his own scandal.

Act I, Scene 4

Cooper remembers that:

> Sonny was quite persistent in his efforts to get me to choose from Shakespeare's *Complete Works*, soon after we arrived in that prison block (B Section). I put this off as much as I could until, months later, he said that he was likely to be removed from Robben Island pending

Running it thus—you'll tender me a fool.
Oph. My lord, he hath importun'd me
with love   110
In honourable fashion.
Pol. Ay, fashion you may call it; go to,
go to.
Oph. And hath given countenance to his
speech, my lord,
With almost all the holy vows of heaven.
Pol. Ay, springes to catch woodcocks! I
do know,   115
When the blood burns, how prodigal the
soul

The kettle-drum and trumpet thus bray out
The triumph of his pledge.
Hor.   Is it a custom?
Ham. Ay, marry, is't;
But to my mind, though I am native here
And to the manner born, it is a custom 15
More honour'd in the breach than the
observance.
This heavy-headed revel east and west
Makes us traduc'd and tax'd of other
nations;
They clepe us drunkards, and with swinish
phrase

Michael K Dingake
3.1.1978

Saths cooper

ANC activist Michael Dingake, and Saths Cooper, a member of the Black Consciousness Movement, signed off on *Hamlet*.

his release. He then left the heavy tome with me, which I promptly placed on the shelf in the cell. A few days later he asked if I had made my choice, which I hadn't, but then had to do it that very night. My dilatoriness had ensured that the famous quotations had been taken, especially in the dramas like *Julius Caesar*, *King Lear* and *Hamlet*. Trawling through the tome, even looking at the comedies and poems, I kept coming back to Hamlet, whose story of deceit, betrayal, madness and corruption had resonance for me, especially against the backdrop of my experiences on Robben Island. The multiplicity of meanings in each thought made me decide on this passage, which reflected what I thought of some of those that I had encountered, especially in prison, and how I viewed their commitment and ability to be 'traduc'd' despite the 'forts of reason'.

'Make us traduc'd ... soil our addition' is sadly what has happened in present-day South Africa, where some of our leaders' antics have compromised us and enabled the younger generations to flee from any inkling of 'struggle' as they pursue crass materialism. In 'it takes from our achievements' was the recognition that there was an emerging tendency to ignobility evinced by some in prison that would distract from the essence of what we were striving for. How often have I not heard people, not only in this country but elsewhere, ask 'Was it worth it?' Our current political shenanigans are best described by 'So, oft it chances in particular men, That, for some vicious mole of nature in them ... take corruption From that particular fault ... To his own scandal.'

Studying Shakespeare tended to be a foisted burden in high school, but involvement in theatre in my mid-teens resulted in an appreciation of his singular contribution to language and the world of words. English has been indelibly impacted by the Bible, Marx, Freud and most certainly by Shakespeare. There is something for 'Everyman' in the latter, whether in tears, laughter or other tribulations and joys.

Moodley also chose from *Hamlet*:

What a piece of work is a man!

How noble in reason! how infinite in faculties!

in form and moving, how express and admirable!

in action, how like an angel! in apprehension, how like a

god!

the beauty of the world! the paragon of animals!

And yet, to me, what is this quintessence of dust?

Man delights not me—no, nor woman neither, though by your smiling you seem to say so.

Act II, Scene 2

Was that Moodley whom Venkatrathnam heard shouting on Robben Island, 'What a piece of work is a man'?

The adherents of *Hamlet* had something in common with Chris Hani: 'I was fascinated with Shakespeare's plays, especially Hamlet … I want to believe I am decisive and it helps me to be decisive when I read Hamlet' (Hani, quoted in *Weekly Mail* 6–10 June 1988).

Michael Dingake chose the words of Polonius in *Hamlet*:

The wind sits in the shoulder of your sail,

And you are stay'd for. There—my blessing with thee! ...

Give every man thy ear, but few thy voice;

Take each man's censure, but reserve thy judgment …

This above all – to thine own self be true,

And it must follow, as the night the day,

Thou canst not then be false to any man.

Farewell; my blessing season this in thee!

Act I, Scene 3

Using the words of Polonius was strange, given the fact that Polonius was a man who accepted the status quo and displayed an overriding loyalty to the ruling class. But Dingake's reading was symptomatic of how Shakespeare was read in ways that made sense to the situation in which prisoners found themselves. Dingake was saying goodbye to a comrade and at the same time offering sage advice.

In a classic case of re-reading a text to make sense of an immediate circumstance, Polonius, while a cynical opportunist, was drawn upon as a model who, once he had made up his mind, would not let anything change it. It was this determination, a single mindedness that appealed to those like Sobukwe who were serving long sentences on the island (Pogrund 2009:246).

The historical plays

O, gentlemen, the time of life is short! …

An if we live, we live to tread on kings.

King Henry IV, Part One, Act V, Scene 2

The series of four plays *Richard II, Henry IV Part I* and *Henry IV Part II*, and *Henry V* were all read with some avidness by the inmates of the single cells, precisely because they spoke to the exercise and fluidity of power and the consequences of acting arbitrarily, as Richard II was to contemplate in the Tower of London.

Joe Gqabi chose from *Richard II*:

Not so; even through the hollow eyes of death

I spy life peering; but I dare not say

How near the tidings of our comfort is.

Act II, Scene 1

Gqabi, the inveterate joker, was a brilliant investigative journalist who made his mark covering the Pondoland revolt of 1960. On the island, Gqabi was quite vocal that there should be no relationship with

Bantustan chiefs and the debates around this issue led to a frosty period with Mandela. As Masondo remembers, Mandela tended to 'interrogate you about your position. I didn't mind that. But my colleague Joe Gqabi took exception to that and would become very angry. As a result, the relationship between them hardened' (SADET 2008:262).

After his release from Robben Island, Gqabi was active in Soweto, especially among the youth of the 1976 generation. In 1978 he left the country. He was to play an influential role in the ANC's think tank in exile. An apartheid assassination squad murdered him in August 1981 in Harare, Zimbabwe.

Mac Maharaj chose the haunting words of Gaunt:

> Where words are scarce, they are seldom spent in vain
>
> For they breathe truth that breathe their words in pain.
>
> *Richard II*, Act II, Scene 1

The sonnets

The sonnet form – artificial and highly stylised – was very popular in the age of Queen Elizabeth I. The sonnet is a fourteen-line lyric poem, traditionally written in iambic pentameter, lines ten-syllables long with accents falling on every second syllable, as in: 'Shall I compare thee to a summer's day?' (Ackroyd 2010:327)

Raymond Mhlaba chose Sonnet 140. This is one of 26 sonnets addressed to a mysterious 'dark lady' (Ackroyd 2010:327):

> Be wise as thou art cruel; do not press
>
> My tongue-tied patience with too much disdain;
>
> Lest sorrow lend me words, and words express
>
> The manner of my pity-wanting pain.

Mhlaba's 'dark lady' was Dideka Heliso. They had a relationship before Mhlaba was arrested, but for three years until his arrest in 1963, she had no idea of his whereabouts.

In the year that Mhlaba signed off on *Shakespeare*, 1977, Dideka came to visit on the island:

> I remember the first time she came to visit ... She was in tears most of the first day. She said very little, as I was dying to hear about my family. I could not even touch her ... It was a dreadful experience. I had so many questions to ask her regarding our children. (They had three children, Mpilo, Nomawethu and Nikiwe.) (Mafumadi 2001:143)

The subsequent visits rekindled the relationship:

> Even though I was growing old in prison, my heart was young. My heart and spirit was longing for hers ... When Dideka came to visit in 1984 I proposed to her. She accepted ... That was one of the best days of my life. (Mafumadi 2001:144)

For two years Mhlaba persisted in requesting permission to get married. On 5 April 1986, they were married at Pollsmoor Prison, with Nelson Mandela and Walter Sisulu as best men: 'At long last we were husband and wife – sixty-eight and sixty-four years respectively' (Mafumadi 2001:143).

All the world's a stage

> Shakespeare grabbed words by the ass and made them shriek and bitch, showing us the range of verbal expression cannot be constrained by the constipated or famished genres of literature. The savage, lyrical and tragic abundance of William Shakespeare continues to be the greatest evidence to support the conviction that ironclad rules have no place in literature. (Fuentes 2005:247)

Venkatrathnam remembers one Christmas the staging of *Coriolanus*, one of his favourite Shakespearean characters. *Coriolanus* cannot be the great politician his mother wants him to be:

because he does not understand the art of adaptation, the art of the chameleon. He is a man of principle, without vanity or airs of importance, vices that he, as a patrician scorns because he has no need to appear a certain way or act in a certain manner other than his own. He *is*. But Coriolanus's integrity endangers the vanity and venality of those around him. He is doomed. He makes everyone uncomfortable. He will remain alone. And he knows this. He will be defeated if he acts, and he will be defeated if he doesn't. (Fuentes 2005:246)

As Feuntes points out, *Coriolanus*:

has given rise to all sorts of ideological confusion. The French Right, in 1933, applauded it and the left prohibited it. The Nazis glorified it and the US occupying army in 1945, banned all performances of it in Germany for a period of eight years. Brecht turned it into a Communist epic about class struggle: the good plebeians versus the bad patricians. (2005:246)

One has a sense that it is the Brechtian version that captured the imagination of Venkatrathnam.

It is uncanny that while *Coriolanus* was making its way through the single cells of Robben Island, at the Lenin Institute in Moscow, Thabo Mbeki was writing about *Coriolanus* to his friends, the Goodings in London. For Mbeki, *Coriolanus* was the epitome of 'truthfulness, courage, self-sacrifice, absence of self-seeking, brotherliness, heroism, optimism'. As Gevisser points out, for Mbeki, *Coriolanus* was 'a revolutionary role model precisely because he was prepared to go to war against his own people who had become 'rabble' … Rome had to be purged of its rot.' The Goodings had a more traditional view, seeing Coriolanus as 'a tyrant driven by hubris!' (Gevisser 2007:xxxix). In 1999, when Gevisser asked Mbeki 'how to escape the fate of Coriolanus', his answer was fascinating, and not a little chilling: 'change society, not yourself' (Gevisser 2007:xl).

When Shakespeare's plays were first made public in the late 16th and early 17th centuries, they were performed in the most rudimentary way:

There was little scenery and no curtains … no way to distinguish day from night, fog from sunshine, battlefield from boudoir, other than through words. So scenes had to be set with a few verbal strokes and the help of a compliant audience's imagination. (Bryson 2009:74)

This was starkly reminiscent of the way Shakespeare's plays were acted out on Robben Island four centuries later:

Our amateur drama society made its yearly offering at Christmas. My thespian career, which had lain dormant since I played John Wilkes Booth while at Fort Hare, had a modest revival on Robben Island. Our productions were what might be called minimalist: no stage, no scenery, no costumes. All we had was the text of the play. (Mandela 1994:441)

Themes

ROSALIND:

Time travels in divers paces with divers persons.

I'll tell you who Time ambles withal,

who Time trots withal,

who Time gallops withal,

and who he stands still withal.

As You Like It, Act III, Scene 2

There are particular themes running through many of the parts of Shakespeare chosen by the prisoners. Time is one of them. Not only the plays of Shakespeare, but also the Sonnets which gave the prisoners the 'sense of time passing, of change of self and an ageing or maturity' (Everett 2008:14). And the confrontation of time:

Yet do thy worst, old Time, despite thy wrong,

My love shall in my verse ever live young.

Sonnet 19

Most of the single cell prisoners were serving lengthy terms and time became pre-eminent. Prison, 'the corrosion of dead time' in Breyten Breytenbach's evocative phrase (1984:212), a point also captured by island inmate Dennis Brutus (1968):

On Saturday afternoons we were embalmed in time

like specimen moths pressed under glass.

Mandela writes of how

[t]ime slows down in prison; the days seem endless ... Watches and timepieces of any kind were barred on Robben Island so we never knew precisely what time it was. We were dependent on bells and warders' whistles and shouts. (Mandela 1994:375)

In August 1982, after being on Robben Island for 18 years, Kathrada wrote:

I once read somewhere that the years roll back quickly in jail, but it is the minutes and hours that drag on at a dreary pace. It is a very apt description of our lives. Ours is a very small world and it is mostly the small things that help to fill the minutes and hours. Small talk, small

events, small interests – these combine to make up a big share of our days and weeks and months. (Quoted in Vahed & Waetjen 2009:79)

Love, tragedy, loneliness. It is this trinity of emotions that were constant companions on the island, along with Shakespeare who so wonderfully captured them.

In fact, throughout the South African twentieth century, the works of Shakespeare were always present. The Bard's words were read and reflected upon, with the writings of Sol Plaatje, the *Drum* decade of the 1950s and among the long-term political prisoners of apartheid from the 1960s. They cut across political lines. Robert Sobukwe, while teaching at the University of the Witwatersrand, told a young white student that

he was writing a Zulu translation of Macbeth. One of his ambitions, he told me, was that he wanted to translate all of Shakespeare into Zulu – to demonstrate the power and beauty of the Zulu language, and because of the power of the original English, which was why he was using Shakespeare. (Pogrund 2009:62)

While in prison with Mandela in 1962, Sobukwe remembers how they talked 'about politics, literature, religion and sport, and shared their books. One such discussion was on the issue of who was the greatest English writer, Shakespeare or George Bernard Shaw' (Pogrund 2009:176). At the service led by Peter Hain for John Harris, a member of the African Resistance Movement (ARM) who was hanged by the apartheid regime in 1965, Shakespeare was recited (Lewin 2011:119).

Dennis Brutus remembers, en route to Robben Island at Leeuwkop Prison,

telling all of Hamlet. As a (continuation) of the Hamlet theme, I also told of Sophocles' *Oedipus*, developing the notion of challenge to authority, and particularly the implied Oedipus complex in Hamlet and its explicit articulation in Sophocles' play; I then used *The Brothers Karamazov* by Dostoevsky to explore the theme further. (Sustar & Karim 2006:66)

A painting made on the island by Sonny Venkatrathnam.

And Zwelonke, who was incarcerated on the island in the mid-1960s, writes of an exchange during a hunger strike (Zwelonke 1989:130):

'The fault, Danny, is not in the stars, but in ourselves,' my friend said.

I looked at him sternly. 'What are you implying? You want to blackleg?'

'No; but I repeat, Danny, the fault is not in the stars, but in ourselves. So noble Cassius would have told noble Brutus. They were speaking of tyranny, remember? It stands to reason who was a tyrant.'

'It was Caesar, of course,' I said.

'So you are Brutus?'

'If I stand on the side of truth.'

'Truth? What truth?' My friend was on the verge of screaming.

'I said quiet there. Bring me your tickets.' It was the span warder. The fool. We gave him the tickets, and continued to discuss Shakespeare. What is wrong with the bum, we thought? Doesn't he understand that we are on strike? How can he punish by hunger when we are on hunger-strike?

The time of the present

Who loses and who wins; who's in, who's out

King Lear, Act V, Scene 3

Venkatrathnam lives in Durban. He is very critical of the new South Africa. For him, the principles that he fought for have been betrayed:

I am bitter, I am bitter. I don't deny that. I think I'm bitter that so many years of struggle seem to have gone down the drain; and we only hope that we can start it again ... we've got the right to vote, we've got the right to free speech ... But we don't have the right to free education; no free medicine; no free housing or anything like that; which is the crux of democracy. If you don't have that, to have the right to vote is meaningless. You can't eat a vote; you can't shelter under a vote ... Freedom means the basic conditions of life need to be addressed. (*Voices of Resistance* 2002)

Yet there is little sense of why the political alternatives that people like Venkatrathnam proposed failed to mount a serious challenge to that of the ANC. What is it about the organisations setting themselves up as more radical and militant than the ANC like the PAC, Apdusa and the black consciousness groupings that saw them splinter and atrophy? Is it not ironic that the people who scream betrayal, '"Treachery, treachery", I cry out thinking of you/comrades and how you betrayed the things we suffered for' (Dennis Brutus, quoted in Sustar & Karim 2006:282) defined the ANC in the first place as short on Left commitments?

A critical account of the Left alternatives to the ANC awaits its historian.

While there might be bitterness, Venkatrathnam also recalls the most rewarding part of his life, lecturing at the University of Durban- Westville throughout the 1990s. He was invigorated by young students eager to learn and they clearly respected Venkatrathnam. Here was a man who had lived the history and politics he was teaching and students appreciated this, as shown in this extract from a poem by student Sipho Buthelezi reveals:

In your voice

There is history

Unfortunately …

It is a history of pain and torture

It is a history of tears and misery

It is a history of the struggle and sacrifice

…

No money can pay your sacrifice

No object can express my appreciation

Blessed is the ground you lie your bones

I will be there to mourn for you

I will testify You were a noble hero

Sipho Buthelezi

The South Africa he fought for will not come in Venkatrathnam's time, but he remains true to his beliefs:

To thine own self be true,

And it must follow, as the night the day,

Thou canst not then be false to any man.

Hamlet, Act I, Scene 3

Sonny Venkatrathnam has taken Michael Dingake's advice seriously.

Some of Sonny Venkatrathnam's sketches on Robben Island.

Sceptreless, free, uncircumscri[bed]
Equal, unclassed, tribeless,
Exempt from awe, worship, de[gree,]
Over himself; just, gentle, [wise:]
Passionless? — no, yet free fr[om]

Prison number: 164/63.
Mzwandile Mdingi, an
Umkhonto we Sizwe soldier.
His favourite Shakespeare is
Macbeth.

MZWANDILE MDINGI

The importance of an ethical education[10]

Ethics was one of the biggest subjects ever taught on Robben Island. What type of ethics do you expect of a political person, regardless of his or her political affiliation? On this remote piece of land, a political prisoner is a personification of the need and the aspiration of an oppressed people. It stands to reason then that the values underpinning the building of that person must reflect what people in the country need and aspire to. So ethics became very important.

Mzwandile Mdingi gained a reputation as a Shakespeare specialist on Robben Island. His knowledge of Shakespeare was nurtured in school and then at the University of Fort Hare:

Shakespeare to start with was a subject which I grew up very much attached to from Lovedale, then at university. Beyond the formal studies it was also an intellectual exercise. Shakespeare for me was brilliantly illustrating the social norms, the social beliefs and the political structures of feudal kingdoms in England prior to the advent of industrialisation. Here the feudal arrangement was based on the monarchies and the churches of England. So it did give an opening or an understanding of the social structure that existed prior to the coming of capitalism into the land of England. So from that perspective I found it intellectually challenging as it gave me deeper insights into an understanding of the social relations which is not only traceable to feudal and monarchic and patriarchal society of Shakespeare's time, but even far back towards primitive societies in England because some of the plays talk about witches and things like that which was still beliefs in Shakespeare's time but they are traceable even before the feudal structure of society.

On Robben Island *Macbeth* was one of the favourites among prisoners. Many prisoners were from the Eastern Cape and the whole notion of witches was a phenomenon they lived with. It is not surprising that Mdingi's favourite lines come from *Macbeth*:

Out, out brief candle!

Life's but a walking shadow

Act V, Scene 5

For Mdingi, it signified that life is short and that a revolutionary must hasten to act if he wants to see change in his lifetime. It was an adage Mdingi personified. He was just 18 years old when he joined MK and 20 when he was incarcerated on Robben Island.

His teaching of Shakespeare combined with a Marxist interpretation of society saw an increasing number of prisoners attending his class.

> Even those guys, some of them could have been matriculants when they were arrested, or in high school. They started becoming interested in furthering their understanding of reading. So when I conducted these English literature classes, even that crowd started attending as a way of opening up their understanding of literature internationally. We ordered books from French, British and Russian authors, and playwrights, this was just for everybody – not only restricted to those who had prescribed books. We had that responsibility to these students. We made them write. From the literacy classes ... when we were sure that they were grasping things, like arithmetic – we had people who could say 'this one'. Those students who were progressing well (the 'this one') were advised to register with correspondence schools.

> This is what happened to our current president. At one stage he happened to be a student in my English class, Jacob Zuma. I said, 'You can do JC [Junior Certificate] now.'

Born in Queenstown in 1944, Mdingi's parents were schoolteachers. His father was a member of the Cape African Teachers' Association (CATA) – an affiliate to the Non-European Unity Movement. His mother died when he was four years old and the family was raised by their father. The Mdingi children attended the local primary school. For his high school years, Mdingi was sent to Lovedale as a boarder. There he completed his Junior Certificate and Matric.

Political consciousness

During his primary school years, the Mdingi family home saw many visitors. The group would drink, talk sports, and discuss the politics of the time. Most of those who frequented the Mdingi household 'later became recognisable in the struggle – from whatever angle'.

> There was Leo Sihlali, he was a teacher and a CATA leader at the time [Sihlali was incarcerated on Robben Island for three years in the mid 1960s]. He was a very astute man ... I remember 'Wycliffe' Tsotsi.

He was an attorney specialising in land disputes. He was also very prominent in the Unity Movement.

One of the leading figures of CATA, an affiliate of the Non-European Unity Movement (NEUM) from the mid 1940s was AC Jordan. Intriguingly, in a 1946 address to the Teachers' League of South Africa, Jordan turns to *The Tempest* to show the limits of the civilising mission:

> If you want a clear picture of the situation in South Africa, you will get it in *The Tempest*. Prospero taught Caliban just sufficient Italian to be able to order him to carry logs of wood. He did not teach him reading and writing because Caliban's knowledge of these was no convenience to Prospero. It just suited Prospero that Caliban thought his master's magic powers lay in the books. All that Caliban could use Italian for was cursing, to which curses Prospero could afford to sit back and listen with the complacency of the elephant because they did not threaten his security. It was only when Caliban refused to obey orders that Ariel was sent to apply cramps, because Caliban's non co-operation threatened Prospero's own security. To Prospero a Caliban remains a Caliban, and has no claim on his respect even if he rises above the level of the drunken butler and the drunken seaman when he hears music. Caliban is the son of Sycorax, the African witch; the drunken Italians, because they are Prospero's own countrymen ... are still better than Caliban. (Quoted in Sandwith 2011:19)

While Mdingi might not have followed his father's friends into the Unity Movement, Jordan's approach of reading Shakespeare in a subversive way was something he was to carry with him onto Robben Island.

And while the overwhelming influence of CATA in the household meant that the ANC 'was hardly spoken about at home', his arrival at Lovedale changed all that. Lovedale was known as the 'Eton of Africa', and as Professor Z. K. Matthews wrote, was 'a wonderland of education, the same kind of education, we thought, which had given the European his all-conquering power, his ability to master the Africans, who were much more numerous, and knew the land so much better' (quoted in Gevisser 2007:89). The 'Eton of Africa', by the time Mdingi arrived, was a place of political debate and ferment. Ahead of Mdingi were the likes of Thabo Mbeki and Chris Hani.

Chris came like a tsunami to talk about the ANC. There were ANC bulletins, ANC weekly newspapers. So, by the time I got to Form 3, Thabo and Chris were doing Form 5 and completing high school. At the time I must have joined the ANC. I remember in 1959 when Thabo launched the African Student's Association, called ASA, and it was the first African Students' Association that was formed. I was part of the organising committee of the group that was selected by Thabo.

For Mdingi, Lovedale was the formative experience of his political life. As a young boy he had seen the ANC from a distance at mass meetings in Queenstown, but at Lovedale he 'met the ANC theoretically'. From Lovedale, Mdingi went to Fort Hare, another incubator of African nationalist thought and activism.

University of Fort Hare

At Fort Hare, Mdingi became acquainted with people such as Andrew Masondo, a lecturer and close friend of Chris Hani. Masondo was an organiser for the ANC – the ANC being banned by this time. The two became very close, and towards the end of 1962, Mdingi was recruited into the structures of Umkhonto we Sizwe (MK). As part of the armed wing of the ANC, Mdingi had to undertake certain operations.

One of those operations was to blow up electricity power lines:

Reconnaissance showed that these power points were supplying the Eastern Cape from East London to Port Elizabeth [PE], and all the towns between, including Queenstown. A decision was taken to blow up these pylons. When we blew them up, the whole of the Eastern Cape was in darkness – from East London to PE. Queenstown. The whole lot. Then we went to our hiding place in our rooms. I remember when I got to my room, the students were outside shouting 'Where is the power? Where is the power?' Unfortunately it was very late at night and I was completely wet. They asked, 'Why are you so wet?' I said that I had left town very late and I got wet on the way from Alice to the campus. That was an MK operation, structured by MK. We were four. But, one of our guys, unfortunately ... I don't know at times how these things happened. Those days it was fashionable for girlfriends

to give a handkerchief with the girlfriend's name embroidered with the name of the boyfriend. One of our guys had this handkerchief ... the handkerchief fell and then that was the clue that led to our arrest ... They took us to Grahamstown Supreme Court. We were tried there. One guy, on a technicality, was discharged and three of us – including Andrew Masondo and Nelson Dick were sentenced. Masondo, being accused number one, got twelve years. I got eight years.[11]

Two-sided education

The common law prisoners sometimes had access to newspapers and passed them on to the political prisoners. However, once the new prison was built and the political prisoners were housed separately, this became more difficult.

In 1964, alongside a number of PAC prisoners, an increasing number of communists and ANC cadres started coming from Port Elizabeth, from Natal, from Johannesburg and Pretoria, and from Cape Town.

As the numbers at Robben Island swelled, Mdingi was among those who realised that many of the prisoners could not read nor write.

We realised that whenever they utilised these privileges of writing their letter allowed once every six months, they used to ask people – PAC, Poqo, ANC, whatever – to help them. They said, 'Can you please help me write this letter?' When a reply would come, they would say, 'Can you please read me this letter?'

Mdingi was troubled that someone else had to read a fellow prisoner's letter, especially in a place where there was already so little privacy. For Mdingi, this was one of the motivations for getting involved in literacy.

Literacy formed one pole and political education the other:

Because some comrades would leave after three, four or five years, depending on the sentence, the rationale was that by the time a man goes out he should be highly politically conscious so as to size up the situation to be challenged. Prisoners realised that the viciousness of the enemy in the late sixties was becoming so harsh and it needed people with very astute political standards. Without that political ammunition they would not be able to manoeuvre in the brutal environment they found themselves. Political education was crucial.

There was also the question of preparing for freedom:

We are going to be free. Here comes freedom. But, when the time comes, these people should be literate and should be able to go and teach their own children – to be able to write, which is a plus in developing the new South Africa. We felt that this was not just to improve the wellbeing of this person, but it was also part of the

Mzwandile Mdingi obtained his degree through Unisa while imprisoned on Robben Island.

project of moving people toward a new South Africa, where literacy and numeracy would be permanent for citizens to apply and exercise their democratic constitutional rights. It was a tool that was necessary for these people's development. So, there was a rationale behind the political and academic education.

Out of these kinds of concerns, according to Mdingi, 'the need for political education; the need for literacy education was born'.

Planning

By the time I left, we could measure the achievement by the results: not seeing anybody asking any other person to read his own letters, or how to write a letter home. That was without the teaching aids which you find in a normal academic school today – desks, boards and computers – it was from brain, mouth-to-ear; and little exercise books.

There was planning to be done:

It was decided that because we were being given the right to study, which came after many hunger strikes, those who are studying Matric upwards, to degree level, should have their own cells ... the first one for students, Matric upwards, in C Section – C1 cell. We were bundled up there. People who were not keen on formal studies were kept in other cells. We first identified people we were going to teach reading and writing to. Then we had to target people who we had to give numeracy training.

Planning had to be done to identify teachers:

We decided that we must identify these people. There were guys who were teachers by profession, but very few. Most of the people who were in the struggle in those days came from hostels and trade unions. A sprinkling of us came from universities but we did not have the theory of teaching – we were not teachers, we were students – but we could teach what we knew. I majored in English and Economics in my degree, so I was identified as one of those to teach English. I completed my degree at Robben Island.

We did not have blackboards and things like that. The way it worked is that when we came back from work, after having a bath, we gave 'students' homework. They wrote stories and then they wrote little compositions and template letters, because the idea was that, at some stage, they would have to write their own letters. They would have to read their own letters. It was like teaching in a primary school – how to write a letter; how to understand it; a little comprehension; how to ask questions based on that; analyse and understand the letter; does this person understand what he is reading? Firstly, it was a Xhosa comprehension, and an English comprehension going together. Initially we had demanded from our side, the ANC's side, that we would like to help across the board – not just ANC people or PAC people. But that had its own problems, because the PAC people – those who were leadership – thought that the teaching would probably permeate into some political education which might influence their people away. That was quite understandable at the time.

We had these three layers: 'Illiterate', High School and Graduate Studies. It was sort of a structured thing. I had the responsibility for some of those 'illiterates', some high school guys and Matric guys – teaching them literature. My specialty was English literature; and doing all plays – Shakespeare, novels, grammar, whatever.

By the time Mdingi's eight years were finished, reading, writing and education were taken very, very seriously – to the envy of the warders.

We would make a point that even when we go to crush stones at the quarry, at lunch time we quickly ate, and we would carry these small books and say, 'Guys, come work here'. And the warders would move around and they got fascinated. They thought, 'How do I, as Warder So-and-So, start now upgrading myself; my education?'

Mdingi emphasises that it was a very difficult environment, designed to oppress and suppress:

The environment could not be said to be highly conducive to study. It was an environment that was suppressed. We tried to perforate the ceiling of suppression. Political education bordered mostly on the history of South Africa, before the whites came, when they came. The usual stuff. And also about when the organisations came into being; why they came; what their problems were; the changing methodology of struggles from past resistance; up to 'why I am struggling?'; the type of person you expect from an armed struggle cadre; and the relation of the cadre with the people – because at the end of the day, they are the liberators and you are just the catalyst. Ethics was one of the biggest subjects ever taught there. What type of ethics do you expect of a political person, regardless of his or her political affiliation? A political prisoner is a personification of the needs and the aspirations of the people. Prison is a type of environment that can breed unethical behaviour, like sodomy, stealing. At some stage, guys who were working in the kitchen stole people's food. Those things might appear simple to a person who is distant from that environment, but it is an environment that can bedevil one's mind. Thus, we had to be on our guard, to never lower our guard in terms of ethics.

We were motivated by the belief that the struggle hasn't come to an end by coming to jail. We are still going to continue struggling even when we come out of jail. We must produce a cadre here who is able to perpetuate the struggle.

So, this type of education, be it political education, was to prepare these persons for the outside world. And, the literacy – the academic education – was also for his personal development for him to be in sync in the new South Africa ... when this new South Africa comes. I think a lot of people in Parliament were in those literacy classes at the time. They could not stand up and address a meeting in English and analyse the situation. But, by the time they got out, they could stand on any platform in the world. What I am trying to say is that through difficult times – the human spirit conquered. I think the South African situation is not unique.

Mdingi was arrested during his second year at university. He obtained his degree through Unisa, while on the island:

But I could not go to the graduation because I was slapped with a three-year house arrest order as soon as I got out of prison. They did not even take me to Queenstown, which was my home. They had opened up a camp about twenty kilometres away from Queenstown

– it was called Ilinge. If you were Xhosa speaking on Robben Island and you were on their list of banned people, more often than not you were taken straight to Ilinge. I remember when we went out – we went from Robben Island – and onto a truck to East London.

Reading on Robben Island

Reading changes our lives, and our lives change our reading.

— Maryanne Wolf, *Proust and the Squid*

Mdingi read more books than he can remember on Robben Island:

The first book I read was by a guy who was not in the communist party. He was socialist-orientated –Jack London – and he had written that book, *The Iron Heel*, which explains the exploitation of workers by capital. It evocatively exposed the life of workers under capitalism, as the title of the book suggests. It impressed me in a very, very big way. It was the first novel ... we went on to read Tolstoy, Maxim Gorky and French novelist, Victor Hugo. And the Americans – mostly guys like John Steinbeck who wrote *The Grapes of Wrath*. And African authors like Chinua Achebe. I also read Engels, *The Origins of the Family, Private Property and the State*. For me this was an important book because as the title implies it showed that the development of the modern family was tied to the development of private property relations. It gave me insights into primitive communism and the role of the state in capitalist societies. To be reading this book inside prison under the noses of the warders only served to increase its value.

For Mdingi, reading was both an escape and an education, allowing him to get a deeper understanding of class politics while asking hard questions about the challenges faced by liberation movements that come to power:

These books allowed me to grow out of the prison walls. I could live through the Russian and French revolutions. Steinbeck's book alerted me to the suffering of the working class in the United States. People forced to be on the move. Apartheid too had brought its dispossession of the land, forcing us to become labour tenants and working on mines deep underground. Achebe alerted me to the challenge of neocolonialism. So reading became both an act of motivation, an act of liberation.

Conviction

People who have got conviction, you can't stop them, no matter how much you torture them, as people were tortured there.

Mdingi lived through that phase of the island when the warders acted with impunity. There were beatings, crude racial baiting and arbitrary sanctions that could take away hard won privileges. Mdingi points to wounds from the island:

You see my ear here? Come closer. You can feel it here. The old people from Robben Island know that. This was a result of being assaulted with pick axes by warders. They said I must push a wheelbarrow and my wheelbarrow's wheel broke and couldn't move forward. I messed it up by telling them, 'You can do whatever you like. One day we are going to rule this country.' Because I said that, they descended on me like a ton of bricks, and this ear was cut off here. We complained to the authorities and they didn't care. They said, 'This fucken Poko'.

These scars I will die with. But they don't make us feel vengeance. I learnt something from [Fidel] Castro's speech in court when he was arrested at the Moncada Barracks in the July 26th Movement in 1953. Castro was separated from his co-accused, who appeared in an army court; and he appeared in an army hospital, alone. The enemy killed a lot of people because they were captured in the mountains. And then Castro, in his nine-hour speech from the dock, said, 'Sir, if you can try me in a hospital surrounded with guns and machine guns, justice is captive.' Then he said, 'Those people who shot my comrades. Killed us. Did all sorts of torture. I hold no vengeance against them, because the blood of comrades who died, if I kill these things it will not repay the blood of those people. The only way we can show gratitude to those comrades who laid down their lives, and the only way which they would appreciate it, if you were to raise them today, is to see a better life for the Cuban people. That is the only way you can repay their lives – by getting a better life. Vengeance and killing these things is not going to take it any step forward.'

For Mdingi,

> Those were the roots of understanding and reconciliation the people talked about: that vengeance does not pay. The only way we can show gratitude to these comrades is by giving what they wished for: a better life for the people. I think those are the things that are still guidelines in life to me.

Self-write

Mdingi is still an avid reader, fuelled by a 'desire to grow intellectually. It is part of my passion, part of my make-up.' He is interested in the Holocaust, an interest sparked by a trip to Germany. Mdingi points out that studying the Holocaust is mandatory in German schools, while in South Africa, the history of apartheid is something the younger generation has very little idea about.

His main interest though is the continuing threat of imperialism. For Mdingi, the fall of the Berlin Wall did not end imperialism. It is still a reality operating in different guises. Imperialism is on the wrong side of history.

Mdingi follows the uprisings in the Arab world and while embracing the struggle unfolding on the streets, he also has reservations:

> There is a lot of spontaneity that is happening there and the uprising, as good as it may be, without a properly structured leadership that knows where it is going can lead to opportunism which can play into the hands of imperialism.

Mdingi learnt many lessons on Robben Island but central is the idea of having conviction and the stamina to pursue that conviction:

> The greatest lesson was how you can stretch the spirit of endurance of people under the most difficult circumstances; if that conviction has not snapped people will not break. It is the conviction that keeps people going. You can beat them. You can do anything. But if the conviction is there, then they will go forward. Once the conviction snaps, they crack. They do all sorts of funny things. That I learnt from Robben Island.

Prison number: 468/64. Ahmed Kathrada, a leading member of the ANC who was tried with Nelson Mandela, signed off on Shakespeare's *King Henry The Fifth*. (Portrait by Jurgen Schadeberg, 1994.)

AHMED KATHRADA

The keeper of books

More than anything else, books helped to keep our minds occupied. By February 1969 I had completed my first degree, and had registered for non-degree courses in anthropology, archaeology, ancient history and English. Both for academic and recreational purposes I read everything I could lay my hands on. (Kathrada 2008(a):236)

Ahmed Kathrada[12] was 35 years old when he began his life sentence on Robben Island in 1964. From a young age in Johannesburg he was involved in politics, coming under the influence of people such as Yusuf Dadoo and I C Meer, leading figures in the Indian Congresses. In 1946, Prime Minister Jan Smuts passed the Asiatic Land Tenure and Indian Representation Act, otherwise known as the Ghetto Act, that gave legal sanction to the segregation of Indians in Natal and curtailed their access to land. The Indian Congresses sought to confront the Act with a passive resistance campaign. It was Kathrada's Matric year. 'But in June, Dr Dadoo, I C Meer and J N Singh [all leading members of the Indian Congresses – the latter two were students at the University of the Witwatersrand] came to fetch me from my classroom to perform some or the other menial task. I never went back' (2008(a):43).

Kathrada was to spend a month in a Durban jail for his activities against the Ghetto Act. It was the beginnings of a journey that saw him involved in the heady mobilisations of the 1950s, as the Indian Congresses built an alliance with the ANC. This journey took him through the 1952 Defiance Campaign (during which he received a nine-month suspended sentence), facing a banning order in 1954, becoming one of the accused in the 1956 Treason Trial, which ended in 1961, house arrest in 1962 and a life sentence on Robben Island.

Ahmed Kathrada was incarcerated for eighteen years on the island. In October 1982 he was transferred to Pollsmoor Prison. He was released in October 1989, having spent 27 years in prison.

When Kathrada decided to study on Robben Island, he wrote to his family:

So when Ma or anyone else starts worrying about me, they must just imagine that I'm not in jail but at university. Only now can I fully appreciate how hasty and unwise I was to give up my studies eighteen years ago. And if I wasn't in jail I wouldn't have had an inclination to go back to the books. So please be very firm with all the children who are neglecting their schoolwork. Do not let them give up. (Kathrada 2008(a):215)

Kathrada finished four degrees while in prison; BA (History/Criminology); BA Bibliography (Library Science/African Politics); and two BA Honours degrees in African Politics and History through Unisa.

According to fellow Robben islander, Laloo Chiba, one of the reasons Kathrada chose to study for a BA in Bibliography was that, 'with a Major in Library Science, it would give him stronger grounds for retaining his position as Librarian of the prison's library' (Chiba, quoted in Venter 2005:15).

The position of librarian also gave him access once a year to other sections of the prison when stocktaking took place.

> The librarians in other sections were also ANC members. We looked forward to the annual stocktaking, when we were brought together to count the books in each section. Virtually unsupervised, we deliberately spent more days than required to count a measly few thousand books. (Kathrada 2008(a):85)

In his *Memoirs,* Kathrada writes about 'three illiterate peasants from the Transkei who had launched an abortive attempt to assassinate Chief Kaiser Mantanzima who were in the same section as the Rivonia trialists and their quest to educate themselves' (2008(a)).[13]

In telling his story he notes that those who had permission to study could only obtain a ballpoint pen by exchanging the old one. After a while the rules were relaxed, motivated by the fact that, as an increasing number of 'prisoners became students, the warders found themselves spending too much of time acting as pen and paper clerks' (Kathrada 2008(a):214). Prisoners were eventually able to get up to six ballpoint pens. Kathrada shared his pens with fellow prisoners.

The three peasants, Kathrada remembers,

> had no money, nor the means of obtaining any, so they could not register as students. It was virtually impossible for us to smuggle pens and paper to them, but someone managed to slip a pencil or a ballpoint pen to one of them. They still had no paper, but then one found a wrapper for Palmolive soap, and started practising to write the alphabet and his own name. He was caught by warders

and placed on spare rations for three meals. Undeterred, the trio used their working hours at the quarry to practise the letters in the sand, and by the time they left the island, all three were literate. (2008(a):214–215)

The collector

> Camouflaged among his university books were ordinary school exercise books which Kathy [Kathrada] filled with quotes from books, magazines and often-smuggled newspapers. While the keeping of such notebooks was not officially allowed, over the years Kathy collected and recorded quotations which had captured his imagination. In the process, he filled seven volumes – six while on Robben Island between 1965 and 1982; and the last volume when he was held at Pollsmoor Prison from October 1982. (Chiba, quoted in Venter 2005:15)

The quotes that Kathrada collected give some indication of the books and other sources he was able to consult. It also gives us some idea of the state of his mind, how he felt about the politics of the time and the conditions they faced. As Venter writes in the preface, the quotes 'reflect his pain, anguish and fear, as well as his characteristic optimism, his principles of justice and humanity and his mischievous sense of humour' (Venter 2005:20–21).

In the first years on the island, the contemplation of life in prison, thoughts of loved ones and the passing of time are all witnessed in Kathrada's quotes. In the extract from Ivan Turgenev, *Fathers and Sons,* his personal status is reflected upon: 'Pavel, the lonely bachelor, was just entering the infinite twilight period of regrets that are akin to hopes, and hopes that are akin to regrets, when youth is over and old age has yet to come' (Venter 2005:40).

The next quote from *The Betrayal* by L P Hartley is a wonderful play on the idea of a clock:

> Often it is a clock, for a clock is not a dead thing, it recollects the past, it has been ticking through the past, it is ticking now and looks

forward to times ahead. A clock lives in the present but it lives in the past and in the future too. It is the ideal present, for it has the freedom of Time's three dimensions. Present ... present ... did the two words come from the same root? (Venter 2005:46)

Reflecting on this quote in his book, *A Simple Freedom,* Kathrada writes of the fact that prisoners were not allowed watches on Robben Island and that:

> especially at work, and during exercise time, the warders used to turn their watches to the other side so we couldn't see the time of day. It was a method of curtailing our exercise time, or making time drag on at work. At the quarry we learnt to guess the time by the shadow of the sun; just as we managed to forecast rain by looking at the clouds over Table Mountain. (Kathrada 2008:105)

And with the arrival of the new commanding officer, Piet Badenhorst, and a shift towards a harsher regime in the early 1970s, 'Kathrada's notebooks took on a more gloomy aspect and, at times, began to reflect on cruelty, and even death' (Venter 2005:47). Kathrada chose a quote from Anna Seghers's *The Seventh Cross*:

> We had a foreboding of the night that was in store for us. The damp autumn cold struck through our blankets, our shirts, and our skin. All of us felt how ruthlessly and fearfully outward powers could strike to the very core of man, but at the same time we felt at the very core there was something that was unassailable and inviolable. (Venter 2005:49)

Was this chosen in the aftermath of an attack by Badenhorst's warders on the single cells?

> One night, a gang of warders carried out an unprecedented raid on the section, wreaking havoc from 1am to 4am. Prisoners had to stand naked with their legs apart and arms outstretched while warders rummaged through their cells ... While he stood shivering against the wall, Walter (Sisulu) could hear the shouts and cursing of the warders and the screams of prisoners being beaten up ... The raid finally came to an end when Govan Mbeki collapsed with severe chest pains. Fikile Bam was so incensed with Mbeki's collapse and distressed that he

was powerless to protect the man whom he regarded as a father that he wept bitterly for the first and only time in his prison experience. (Sisulu 2004:321–322)

It was during this period, the early 1970s, that Kathrada was sentenced to six months' solitary confinement for trying to send a note to Andimba Toivo ja Toivo of the South West Africa People's Organisation (Swapo). He was only allowed toiletries and the Bible.

Kathrada read the Bible with keen interest and selected a number of pieces from it (as quoted in Venter 2005:61,62) that are pregnant with meaning:

> Knowest thou not this of old, since man was placed
>
> upon earth,
>
> That the triumphing of the wicked is short, and the
>
> joy of a hypocrite but for a moment?
>
> Job 20:4–5

and

> We are troubled on every side, yet not distressed; we are
>
> perplexed, but not in despair; persecuted, but not forsaken;
>
> cast down, but not destroyed.
>
> 2 Corinthians 4:8

Laloo Chiba contrived to smuggle to him a copy of Thomas Mann's *The Magic Mountain*. The book's setting is a sanatorium in the Swiss mountains. It is a place haunted by sickness and death. In his *Memoirs,* Kathrada writes:

> I should have abandoned the book at an early stage, but the more I read about the illnesses of the characters, the more I was drawn to them, until not only did they have my total sympathy, but I

found myself experiencing the very symptoms Mann described. My persistent requests to see a doctor must have prompted an entry in my prison file, which I came across years afterwards: 'Ahmed Kathrada is just a frustrated man who has lost his objectivity and is lodging all kinds of petty complaints instead of accepting his position and trying to make the best of it'. (2008(a):252)

Venter's last section is dated from 1982 to 1989 and is titled 'Freedom is coming'. Surprisingly, no mention is made in the book of how Kathrada's selections start to reflect words such as compromise and dialogue as the three following quotes (in Venter 2005:122–123) show:

> The word 'negotiate' was first used in recorded time by Shakespeare in 1599 in *Much Ado about Nothing* – 'Let the eye negotiate for itself, and trust no agent.' The root of the word is two Latin terms meaning without ease. (Prof Geoff Hughes (Wits), *Sunday Star Review* 30 July 1989, quoted in Venter 2005:122)

> A poor peace is better than a good quarrel
>
> > Russian proverb

> Don't you realise? – discussion, dialogue, call it what you will is the one thing they dare not allow
>
> > Andre Brink, *A Dry White Season*

When asked about books that made an impression upon him, Kathrada points to Anne Frank, the young Jewish girl who hid from the Nazis in Amsterdam during the Second World War. In this confined space she kept a diary from 12 June 1942 to 1 August 1944. It included an often honest rendering of the people who were cramped into a small space with her and details of the trials of confinement and the challenges of a teenage girl entering adolescence. For Kathrada,

> Anne Frank represented courage. We managed to smuggle her *Diary* in, and it made a huge impact … In some ways her situation was similar to ours. But, of course hers was much worse … she faced certain death. We admired the courage and maturity of this young girl, as well as the heroism of the Dutch family who harboured the Franks' at extreme risk to themselves. (Kathrada 2008:91)

Kathrada also notes that Nehru's autobiography made a lasting impression on him. During his earliest days on Robben Island, Kathrada noted this excerpt about fear and reality from Nehru's *Discovery of India*: 'fear builds its phantoms which are more fearsome than reality itself, and reality when calmly analyzed and its consequences willingly accepted loses much of its terror' (Venter 2005:33).

Ahmed Kathrada had two faithful companions through his many periods of imprisonment – the *Oxford Book of English Verse* and *The Complete Works of Shakespeare*. Both books were with him at Christiana Prison, Marshall Square, the Fort and Modderbee. When he was preparing to begin his life sentence on Robben Island, two 'loyal companions, the *Oxford Book of English Verse* and *The Complete Works of Shakespeare*' (Kathrada 2008(a):193) were among his meagre possessions.

Shakespeare was always close to Kathrada's heart. When he was detained in 1963 after being captured at Rivonia and kept in solitary confinement, he spent 'hours and hours recalling and giving voice to a repertoire that ranges from 'Humpty Dumpty' to lines from *Macbeth*, *Hamle*t and the *Merchant of Venice*' (Kathrada 2008(a):11).

According to Kathrada, 'somehow Shakespeare had something to say to us' on Robben Island, though he once tried to 'argue that Shakespeare was a racist' (Sampson 1999:233). He laughed as he recounted that little did he know he was talking to the likes of Dennis Brutus and Neville Alexander, who were steeped in literature and they quickly 'put me in my place'.

Kathrada chose the following words from *Henry V* in Sonny Venkatrathnam's Shakespeare:

> KING:
> Once more unto the breach dear friends, once more;
> Or close the wall up with the English dead.

In peace there nothing so becomes a man

As modest stillness and humility;

But when the blast of war blows in our ears,

Then imitate the action of the tiger:

Stiffen the sinews, summon up the blood,

Disguise fair nature with hard-favour'd rage;

Then lend an eye a terrible aspect;

Let it pry through the portage of the head

Like the brass cannon; let the brow o'erwhelm it

As fearfully as doth a galled rock

O'erhang and jutty his confounded base,

Swill'd with the wild and wasteful ocean,

Now set the teeth and set the nostril wide;

Hold hard the breath, and bend up every spirit

To his full height.

Act III, Scene 1

While Kathrada does not remember choosing the quote, it is an interesting choice given Kathrada's own history with MK. He had terminated his membership of MK in the first half of 1962 because he felt that, in addition to the fact that his capabilities were with political rather than military work, he was also concerned about the lack of 'elementary security' by some members of MK, as well as a cavalier approach adopted by the MK in its choice of targets (Kathrada 2008(a):142–143).

Kathrada's choice also reflects that, while Sonny Venkatrathnam was leaving the island and Kathrada was serving a life sentence, the struggle for freedom was unrelenting. Kathrada was aware that the experience of betrayal (Sonny's close comrades had given evidence against him) and

the experiences of prison could leave permanent scars but he remains encouraging and optimistic, insisting 'once more unto the breach ... once more'.

The mystery of *Indian Delights*

> Towards the end of 1968 the rigid regulations on reading matter were relaxed slightly. I had signed up for some of the publications immediately, including *Panorama* ... as a government publication it was supposed to be given to us uncensored, but before long I found large chunks missing from my copy ... I lodged a complaint with Major Huisamen ... The offending pages had been excised because they featured photographs of young women in bikinis. I was momentarily dumbfounded, but quickly recovered and pointed out that I was studying anthropology and that my textbooks contained photographs of completely naked women, let alone in swimsuits. 'Those must be Bantu women', said the major, and there the matter rested. (Kathrada 2008(a):235)

One gets an all too rare a glimpse into the prisoners' quest to study and acquire reading material, through a series of letters between Ahmed Kathrada and Zuleikha Mayat, 'a self-described house-wife', between 1979 and 1989 (Vahed & Waetjen 2009:1). The initial stimulus for the epistolary correspondence was Kathrada writing a letter of condolence to a friend, Abdulhak 'Bis' Bismillah, on the death of Bismillah's sister, Sakina Bibi Mall, and brother-in-law, Dr Mohamed Mayat, in a car accident. Zuleikha, the widow of Mohamed Mayat, receives the letter in the absence of 'Bis' and replies to Kathrada. And so begins a ten-year correspondence.

The first time Zuleikha Mayat mentions sending a copy of *Indian Delights* to Kathrada is in her very first letter, dated 19 May 1979. Mayat receives a letter dated 4 September 1979 about two books that she had sent to Kathrada, an 'Urdu into English' dictionary and a recipe book (*Indian Delights*), from a Major J W Harding. Both books were rejected, though Harding does commend Mayat for her 'interest in the prisoners and their welfare' (Vahed & Waetjen 2009:33). Kathrada responds to this news with a letter to Mayat dated 21 June 1980: 'Perhaps Tolstoy can be forgiven when in desperation he exclaimed that civil servants had regulations instead of hearts' (Vahed & Waetjen 2009:35). In 1981, Mayat solicits the help of Mahmoud Rajab, a member of the government-appointed President's Council. Rajab wrote to H J Coetsee to find support so that the two books could be given to Kathrada. The request was denied (Vahed & Waetjen 2009:54).

Zuleikha Mayat, a friend of Ahmed Kathrada, sent him her *Nanima's Chest*. This book on Indian antique costumes was allowed by the prison censors after a lengthy appeal by Mayat to the authorities to have this and other books delivered to Kathrada.

In a letter dated 30 June 1982, Mayat is still at it, writing to Colonel Scott:

> I have tried during the past two years, to send some books to one of the prisoners at Robben Island. Viz; Ahmed Kathrada, but have met with little success.
>
> The books are:
>
> 1) An English translation of the Holy Quran
>
> 2) *Nanima's Chest* which is a book on Indian Antique costumes in the possession of Indian South Africans.
>
> 3) *Indian Delights* which is a cookery book on Indian Dishes. (Vahed & Waetjen, 2009:67)

On 30 August 1982, Scott writes back that while permission for the first two books on the list was granted 'at no cost to the state', *Indian Delights* was not to be allowed (Vahed & Waetjen 2009:76). Mayat's persistence in wanting to send a cook book to a person who was living on the most meagre of diets is interesting in itself. At the same time, there seems to be no particular reason that *Indian Delights* was singled out. The fact that even Rajab could not sway the authorities points to the seriousness with which this was regarded. Attempts to unlock the 'revolutionary potential' of *Indian Delights* were in vain.

The receipt *of Nanima's Chest* sees Mayat write to Kathrada for:

> Honest criticism ... Many young persons have felt that Indian roots must be shed in Africa and one should not harp about past traditions and heritage. My view is we can enrich each other's cultures by absorbing other trends ... Close yourself off like the Afrikaner and you remain with Boerewors en Jan Pierewit[14] [Pierewiet] liedjie [small ballad, song]. Political assimilation will lead to social and cultural (assimilation) in its own time. (Vahed & Waetjen 2009:85)

Kathrada writes back on 30 January 1983 from Pollsmoor Prison. He had been transferred to Pollsmoor on 21 October 1982. Kathrada begins his letter by explaining in stark language why he would probably not be able to pursue a master's degree:

I'd like to do an MA if I get through, but there is a regulation which stipulates that MA studies can only be allowed to prisoners who have two years or less of their sentences remaining. As you know I'm doing life for which there is no ceiling, so it seems an M A will be out. (Vahed & Waetjen 2009:86)

Kathrada then addresses the issue of *Nanima's Chest,* writing that he has to be brief, and begins by quoting a young prisoner (whom he does not name at the time of writing):[15]

He was simply ecstatic. His comments were of special significance because he hails from Soweto; he is highly intelligent and articulate; and most important he is young and came to jail after 1976. In fact I had arranged with him to write out his comments. Then, I had given the book to my fellow librarian, and he circulated it throughout the prison. I had just begun to get feedback when I was removed. Let me assure you that there was not a single negative comment. Not a single person, no matter what his persuasion, made remarks about discarding past traditions and heritage. My own views are best expressed in a passage I read by Gandhi where he says: 'I want the culture of all lands to be blown about my house as freely as possible. But I refuse to be blown off my feet by any.' My main criterion for judging questions of this nature is whether they promote sectionalism. *Nanima's Chest* should give no cause for concern for any anxiety on this score. (Vahed & Waetjen 2009:87)

Nanima is Urdu for grandma. The book is a slim volume that catalogues Indian heirlooms in private households. At one level it is surprising that the book evoked such interest on the island. But the book needs to be seen in a broader context of race, ethnicity and culture. As Andrew Verster writes in the introduction to *Nanima's Chest*, '(t)his book is important as it makes this heritage accessible and in a small way helps break down barriers and counteract the notion that culture can be divided. Emphatically it says that these are ours, for us all to enjoy' (Mayat 1981:7).

Mayat writes that one of the reasons for producing the book was that 'future generations will remember, and cherish their roots and their heritage and look on them with pride' (Mayat 1981:13).

Indian Delights, a book edited by Zuleikha Mayat on cookery, was not passed by the censors.

This approach of 'racial groups' keeping their traditions and distinctions fitted with the ANC position of different political organisations for the apartheid-designated 'races'. Despite this, the ANC and the prisoners in general looked beyond 'race' or, as in the words of Kwedi Mkalipi, they saw themselves 'as one family facing a common enemy'.

This did not mean there were no tensions, both between and internal to organisations. Kathrada was shocked when some members within the ANC sought to exclude non-Africans from the right to vote in an internal organisational debate, reflecting that it was 'the most unfortunate and embarrassing period' of his time on the island (Kathrada 2008:291).

The festering sore of 'race' led to a legendary debate between Neville Alexander and Nelson Mandela (see chapter on Neville Alexander).

Access to information

> Common-law prisoners were our main sources of news. They could get newspapers and could even lay their hands on radios … We never handled the money sent by our families to pay for study material and toiletries, so we bartered such items as soap, toothpaste and cigarettes in exchange for newspapers. As soon as the common-law prisoners realized how desperate for news we were, they turned the arrangement to their greater advantage, trading single pages rather than the entire publication. (Kathrada 2008:246)

In a letter dated 12 June 1983, Kathrada informs Mayat that he was not given permission to do a Master's and so had registered for an Honours degree in African Politics (Vahed & Waetjen 2009:90).

On 10 June 1985, Mayat writes once again to prison officials to get permission to send Indian Delights to Kathrada (Vahed & Waetjen 2009:143).

On 14 June 1987, Kathrada writes to Mayat:

> About ordering a copy of Indian Delights, I'm afraid it is not going to be possible. When the new concessions were made we had hoped that there would be some relaxation on the question of books. But

there wasn't. So at present it seems that I'll have to wait until I come out of jail one day before I can peruse the book. (Vahed & Waetjen 2009:216–217)

Meanwhile, Kathrada informs Mayat that he was reading Fiela se Kind and Die Swerfjare van Poppie Nongema (Vahed & Waetjen 2009:237).

Things eventually started to look brighter for Kathrada. On 25 March 1989, he wrote to Mayat that he could proceed with an MA (Vahed & Waetjen 2009:263). Then on 15 July 1989, he informed Mayat that he had finally received the copy of Indian Delights (Vahed & Waetjen 2009:269).

It was a ten-year struggle, but Kathrada was hardly given a chance to sample the taste of Indian Delights. By the end of the year, Kathrada would be a free man.

Kathrada emphasises the fact that prisoners would do anything for information. They began to receive newspapers from September 1980 and were also able to watch movies.

In September 1981, Kathrada wrote to Mayat about missing the presence of children and how he and his fellow prisoners sought to fill this vacuum through books and films:

> Occasionally we do see, and in some instances some of us have actually touched, a child. In the absence of this, one wallows in reading about children in letters and books, in talking about them, and in films. Films such as Heidi, The Champ, Kramer vs Kramer, iLollipop proved to be among the more popular ones. (Vahed & Waetjen 2009:52)

With the move to Pollsmoor, Kathrada's writing takes a more strident form. Information from the 'outside world' was increasing and through his letters, he was in a sense writing back. In 1985, Kathrada wrote to Mayat that he had found a number of historical inaccuracies and errors in the various newspapers he had read: 'The trouble with this type of thing is that, in time to come, researchers will use such newspaper articles as their primary sources – in the process they will perpetuate inaccuracies' (Vahed & Waetjen 2009:140).

In the mid-1980s, with the Rivonia grouping now ensconced at Pollsmoor Prison, they were allowed to watch television:

> For sheer entertainment my favourite programme is the Cosby Show. I stress entertainment, because one cannot look upon the series as a reflection of the reality of the socio-economic conditions of Black people in America ... But I don't want to fall into the groove of seeking a social message in every film, novel, cartoon or comic. (Vahed & Waetjen 2009:203)

Mayat upbraids Kathrada in her reply:

> The Cosby show is excellent. Forget the colour and concentrate on the family that talks, and communicates and retains its sense of humour – as such the show cannot be faulted. If I were to analyse everything I enjoy, even my *Indian Delights* would choke me, for while I am eating, millions are starving. (Vahed & Waetjen 2009:207)

Kathrada is half chastened:

> Regarding the Cosby show, there can be no quarrel in general, with your advice that one should concentrate on the family situation ... Perhaps the motive of the producers was to highlight these. But I still believe that one must always bear in mind the affluence and general lifestyle of the Cosby's is not representative of the typical American Black family. Having made this point, I assure you that I thoroughly enjoy every episode; it remains No.1 on my list. (Vahed & Waetjen 2009:212)

Memory

> In prison one needs to assert little freedoms to preserve the vision of 'greater freedom.' When I was finally released on 15 October 1989, I took with me many cardboard cartons. The prized possessions were my *Oxford Book of English Verse* and Shakespeare's *Complete Works*, which I had managed to keep with me through six prisons, as well as nine hundred carbon copies of letters I had written and an equivalent number received. There were also seven notebooks of quotations. One of the reasons I had kept them was that whenever I jotted a quotation down it simply made me feel better. (Kathrada 2008:49)

While Kathrada hung on to his precious companions as he prepared for the outside world after almost three decades, it did not provide a toolkit for dealing with the changes. His *Memoirs* displays much of Kathrada's sense of humour, especially when he writes of adjusting to the outside world after his release:

> [E]verywhere I turned, there were gadgets and electronic devices ... I had never seen before, each with a name that wasn't in my vocabulary: Walkman and beeper and steering lock and laser printer ... As for language usage, efficiency aids and jargon, I recall how activists in the 1940s and the 1950s managed to organize ... the Defiance Campaign ... the Congress of the People without the benefit of consultants, events organizers, brainstorming sessions, strategic workshops, think tanks, keynote addresses, organograms, and so on. I have still not adjusted fully to these, and I suspect my comrades are exasperated whenever I question the necessity of these so-called aids. (2008(a):347)

While humorous, it is also haunting. Men who were cut off for some three decades were thrust into the role of leading negotiations with the apartheid government. Globalisation had accelerated, new international multilateral organisations were trespassing national boundaries and the Berlin Wall had collapsed. As the ANC searched for economic models, ironically it was consultants and think tanks that muscled in. One only has to follow the development of the Growth, Employment and Redistribution (Gear) programme – the economic programme of the ANC government – by a small group of economists, to see how quickly a stranglehold was created by 'experts' from on high. One of the participants in the drafting of Gear, Stephen Gelb, remarks that 'this was "reform from above", with a vengeance, taking to extreme the arguments in favour of insulation and autonomy of policymakers from popular pressures' (Gelb 1999:16–17).

While his memoirs were first published in 2004, ten years after the historic elections, Kathrada has surprisingly little to say about the negotiations process, the compromises that had to be made and the effects of scaling back transformative economic policies.

Neither does he reflect on the issue of 'race' in post-apartheid South Africa, an issue that hurt so much on the island. Rather he looks to the decision to give South Africa the World Cup as a time:

> when we walked tall. We were unwaveringly proudly South African ... the spontaneous outpouring of celebration following FIFA's decision, the solidarity of pride and unity evoked by a sporting event should serve as a shining example to black and white alike. (2008(a):371)

Was the sharp, incisive mind of prison dulled by the challenges of power and *realpolitiek*? It says something though that the Ahmed Kathrada Foundation has as its mission, 'deepening non-racialism'.

Kathrada served as Nelson Mandela's parliamentary counsellor in the Office of the President. He retired from parliament in 1999.

Kathrada was to play an important role in keeping memory alive, serving as chairperson of the Robben Island Council. Throughout his prison years, Kathrada was earnest about the importance of historical facts and righting the wrongs of colonial and apartheid history. In one of his quotes, he chooses these words from Nehru's *Discovery of India*: 'History is almost always written by the victors and conquerors and gives their view' (Venter 2005:57).

As Mandela writes in the foreword to Kathrada's memoirs, after being released from prison Kathrada 'characteristically, became involved in archival, historical and legacy projects about the liberation movement' (Kathrada 2008(a)).

There is an irony here, considering Nehru's words. One must ask how much of South African liberation history has become the history of the ANC? The history of the victors written in a unilinear way that ends in ultimate redemption? And how much of that history has become the sanitised version?

One of the quotations that Kathrada jotted down in his island notebook was from Milton:

> As good almost kill a man as kill a good book. Who kills a man kills a reasonable creature, God's image, but he who destroys a good book, kills reason itself, kills the image of God, as it were, in the eye. Many a man lives a burden to the earth; but a good book is the precious lifeblood of the master spirit, embalmed and treasured up on purpose to a life beyond life'. (Quoted in Kathrada 2008:84)

In his flat in Killarney, Johannesburg, there are books marked with yellow stickers. Kathrada is still a collector, he still values the power of books.

If we ~~all~~ were judged according to the consequences of all our words & deeds, beyond the intention And beyond our limited understanding of ourselves & others, we should be all condemned.
T.S. Eliot. 1965.

"What need the bridge much broader than the flood?" Much Ado About Nothing.

=

The loathsome mask has fallen, the man remai Sceptreless, free, uncircumscribed, but man Equal, unclassed, tribeless, and nationles Exempt from awe, worship, degree, the king Over himself; just, gentle, wise; but man Passionless? – no, yet free from guilt or pain.
L.T.

Prison number: 369/64. Marcus Solomon, a member of the National Liberation Front. The transcription is Solomon's and appears as a handwritten note at the back of Shakespeare's *The Complete Works* that he took off the island with him. 'L.T.' stands for Leon Trotsky.

MARCUS SOLOMON

The teacher who keeps learning

It is in the very nature of your activity or in the incarceration ... you want to study more, know more, and you have to write ... when people come together because of their political ideals ... they always do things, because struggle is about changing yourself intellectually and emotionally, and changing your material conditions. So when we got to the island, there was always a discussion around what we stood for; what is the nature of our politics? We were always busy studying, arguing, discussing, debating, and trying to find answers – to solve the challenges we were facing. How did other people get liberation? What can we learn from history? So, in a big group like that – in the general section of the jail – there were different levels of awareness; different levels of understanding and experience.

When Marcus Chinasamy Solomon[16] speaks about reading and education, the touchstone and inspiration of his continuing resolve is Robben Island, nearly three-and-a-half decades after he was released. Solomon was arrested in 1963 and imprisoned on the island from April 1964 to April 1974.

Solomon was born in Grahamstown. His mother, according to apartheid categories, was classified coloured and his father Indian. After a brief sojourn in Durban the family settled in Port Alfred. Solomon was sent to Cape Town so he could finish his Standard 9 and Matric.

Caught up in the acrimony and splits within the Non-European Unity Movement, Solomon was among those who formed the National Liberation Front (NLF).

While he was arrested for being a member of the NLF, most of his trial appeared under the Yu Chi Chan Club (YCC). It was called that because when the cops first found out about Solomon and his cohorts, they discovered on them some material about the *YCC Club – Yu Chi Chan*, also the title of Mao Zedong's book on guerrilla warfare:

[W]e became known by that name. But it was never an organisation. It was just a study group on guerrilla warfare. Guerrilla warfare at that time was the form of struggle taking place in many different countries. It is an old form of warfare from ancient times – of Spartacus, et cetera. But in modern times the Chinese, the Spanish, the Cubans, the Algerians, the Mozambicans, and all those countries conducted guerrilla warfare. It was a modern form of liberation struggle.

While their activity around armed struggle was at the level of study groups, Solomon's group was charged with attempting to overthrow the state by means of arms.

> It is treason – conspiring to commit these things. That is what I went to jail for. I spent ten years on Robben Island and when I was there I spent most of my time in the general section or the communal section. I went to jail with people like Neville Alexander, Fikile Bam, Leslie van den Heyden, Don Davis, Lionel Davis, Elizabeth Van den Heyden, Dorothy Alexander, Dulcie September, Doris van der Heerden.

The latter four, given that Robben Island was a male preserve, were detained on the mainland, eventually ending up in Kroonstad Prison.

Political consciousness

Solomon's early political influences began in 1957 when he attended Trafalgar High School, which, at that time, was a hotbed of political discussion and debate. There were few teachers who were actively involved in the Teachers' League of South Africa, an affiliate of the Non-European Unity Movement.

At school his teachers instilled in him a sense of non-racialism:

> Black people called each other 'Kaffir', 'Coolie', 'Boesman', and all that. They showed us that there was a healthier way of thinking about life. You are human beings. There is no such a thing as different races – only one race, and that is the human race. We all basically come from the same roots. Even though we aren't equal, we need to strive for this equal society where people can live in peace with each other, living as equals

Soon enough, Solomon was introduced to ideas of socialism, communism, Marxism, and how to look at life. In class, and especially through his history lessons, he began to study past struggles – starting with the French Revolution, with its slogans of 'equality, fraternity and liberty' – and he was also encouraged to read novels like the *Tale of Two Cities* by Charles Dickens.

When we studied the 1848 revolts, we had to read Émile Zola's *Germinal*, the famous one about working class life and struggles. In fact, I eventually fell in love with Zola and read all his novels.

His teachers also introduced him to the struggle for equality, brotherhood of people, and the whole idea of how resources should be used.

> Why is there poverty? Why the rich are there? It wasn't long before I became very interested in all these things. And then we had the New Era Fellowship, where we used to have lectures in Cape Town. I stayed at Zonnebloem College in Cape Town – a very famous place … A school set up by the British government.

Solomon went to Hewat Teachers' Training College in 1959 because he did not have enough money to go to a university, although he got an exemption. He joined the Cape Peninsula Students' Union (CPSU).

Prison

> Today, history is the story of the victorious – those who won; those who think they have won – and, from the start of the discussion, this has to be kept in mind. Also, the response of the authorities. Reading was banned. No reading, except the Bible. We were always on the lookout for reading the news, newsletters or newspapers.

When he arrived on Robben Island in 1964 as a convicted prisoner, Solomon was already familiar with the place and knew some of the prisoners. This was because the male members of the NLF accused had been moved from the mainland to the island during the trial – the authorities had accused them of attempting to escape. When Solomon first got to the island, the majority of prisoners were PAC, but soon thereafter an increasing number of ANC members started to arrive.

Solomon arrived in the midst of discussions around literacy training.

> So almost from the time we got there – and others had been there – there was already discussion around literacy. But, because it was very difficult to get hold of reading material, from the start we struggled for reading materials, for food, over the living conditions, and over

the right to study. There were different levels of skilled and educated people: lawyers, doctors, professors – like Andrew Masondo, a lecturer at Fort Hare. Neville Alexander was a doctor of philosophy, and a teacher, too. Others could not read or write at all. I was trying to make sense of how to redress this issue. At the same time if you had a book – any book – and you were found with the book or any reading material, you were in trouble

Conditions on the island were brutal and warders felt they could act with impunity. So the first struggle was a defensive struggle.

> [Y]ou wanted to stop the assaults and ill treatment of prisoners. We struggled to get recognition as political prisoners. But, because South Africa was not a signatory to the Geneva Convention or something called the 'protocol governing the treatment of political prisoners or soldiers', they treated us like ordinary prisoners. But we took advantage of that [non recognition] because, in terms of the Prisons Act of South Africa, all prisoners had to be encouraged to study ... we turned the whole thing on its head – or we put it back on its feet: the right to food, the right to study, the right to learn, living conditions that are universally acceptable. And from the start, as with education, we started our literacy programme.

There was a tremendous challenge to teach people to read and write in English.

> We then made a very important decision that people must first become skilled in their mother tongue. I always say that we became familiar with the Paulo Freirean approach before we actually became aware of his works. It is very fascinating. Some prisoners were very old already. I remember when I was found guilty of something and I was actually isolated – segregated for six months – and they took away all my studies. When I came out [from the segregated section] I couldn't go back to the study section. They took away all my studies. Then I used that time – when I was in that section, where there were no study facilities – to teach literacy to my cell mates, mostly guys from the Transkei, both ANC and PAC. I did the basic stuff.

> One chap, William Mabongo, I will never forget. He was involved in the 1946 miners' strike on the Rand. He was a very eager learner and

had a very clear, and in many ways, brilliant mind. But, he had only managed to attend school for a short while and wanted to improve his reading and writing skills. Comrade William Mabango was an old man. He never received any visitors. I felt so sorry and we became very close afterwards.

Solomon taught Mabango to read and write. But at the same time he learnt much from Mabango, about the early struggles of the working class, the constant interplay between tradition and new ways of living on the mines and how to conduct oneself under conditions of duress. Those who had previously worked on the mines, Solomon remembers, were a constant source of knowledge as they had learnt the art of survival under despotic and authoritarian conditions.

Born out of these experiences, Solomon came to reject the whole process of teaching as a one-way street of knowledge dissemination. For Solomon, it is important to create an environment in which you can be both learner and teacher.

Learning and teaching

> Robben Island became a place where people learnt and studied a lot – that is why there is a poster: 'Robben Island is our University'. Have you seen that poster there on the island? Have you heard about it?

As Solomon remembers, it was the PAC's Johnson Mlambo, who was the first person to eventually get permission to continue his studies. The authorities made a separate study cell. Solomon remembers other prisoners passing the C-Section where he had all his books – novels and plays. 'We were so impressed and so desirous and envious of this guy.'

> One of the conditions for Mlambo being allowed to study was that he could not lend his books to other prisoners – that is why they put him in a cell all on his own. Eventually others got that permission to study. Mainly the guys were doing Matric and university studies. This was followed by more prisoners being allowed to get certificates for Standard 6, and Standard 8.

OUR UNIVERSITY!

Robben Island

PUBLISHED BY AZANIA (SOUTH AFRICA) LIBERATION SUPPORT COMMITTEE, BM BOX 4865, LONDON, WC1N 3XX   ORIGINAL DRAWING BY KEN SPRAGUE, 1983

That process snowballed and we eventually got books and material so that we could set up a special cell for people who were studying, and have them all staying together. The prison authorities set up a special section within the administration to ensure that people were not abusing this study facility. Of course, they also used it as a tool of punishment. They said it is a privilege, and a privilege is something you can give and something you can take it away at any time.

We said, 'No ways. You can't allow us to study, register for university, buy books, and then you just come along and punish me and take my studies away because I did something wrong. No. Excuse me.' We checked [the laws governing prisons] and we took them to court. We said, 'Although it is privilege, you can't take it away at any time. It is a privilege that the Prisons Act makes provision for'. Others got the right to study and got books. Eventually we had to structure our literature programme and our study programme. We also had a literary society that encouraged short story writing. Tshwete [Steve] was the chairperson of that.

Tshwete wrote beautiful Xhosa. He wrote a novel. I don't know what eventually happened to that novel. Very interestingly, we eventually got a library. We started setting up academic study groups – Matriculants, maths, science, geography, history, et cetera. Because I was a trained primary school teacher, I was part of the primary school programme – literacy and post-literacy study programme. There were two sections. There was the general section, where the majority of the prisoners used to stay; and there was a segregation section, where Nelson Mandela, Walter Sisulu, Neville Alexander and those people were kept. Generally they were more educated – doctors, lawyers, et cetera.

In our section, there were very big differences in literacy. Most of the chaps came from the Transkei and couldn't read and write, so we had a very big literacy and post-literacy programme. People wanted to read and write English, but it took a very long

This poster was published by the Azanian (South African) Liberation Support Committee in London in 1983. Reproduced by courtesy of the Ken Sprague Fund.

time. After long discussions, we decided what is important is mother-tongue literacy.

The history and geography of struggle

Why are you against the Freedom Charter? Why are you a member of the Pan-Africanist Congress? Why are you for the United States of Africa? Why do you say 'Africa for the Africans?' What about the other so-called population groups? What do you understand by the distribution of wealth? Because the whites already have wealth and you want to distribute and still share with them. What is this thing of freedom? Freedom for whom? How do you get freedom? What makes us people? Must we just study? What about other things?

Solomon, who taught primary school Geography and History was very taken with the Vietnamese war against the Americans. While Mao's insurgency and the Bolshevik Revolution were still the mainstay of discussion, with a rudimentary knowledge of the Cuban struggle, prisoners showed an increasing interest in Vietnamese guerrilla warfare. Solomon was keen to talk about the Vietnamese war because for him it starkly showed the power of human action to prevail over overwhelming odds. It also brought his knowledge of history and geography together:

It was about human beings being important. That was the philosophy. The Americans would be depending on these powerful weapons. I remember the first Mirage jet that flew over Vietnam was shot down by a heat-seeking missile which was set off by six Vietnamese soldiers. It cost about six billion rand to produce at the time. The Americans spent this amount to develop the plane. It could escape radar detectors. The whole philosophy of the Vietnamese struggle was to develop, and depend on human beings. Change comes through people, not technology. We got hold of *Time* magazine with a beautiful map of southeast Asia. This stimulated discussions about the Vietnam War. There were also classes on the history of Africa's struggle to be free of imperialist interests.

The very positive thing the PAC contributed to our struggle was the need to unite Africa. The ANC had a lot of experience with the Soviet Union. The ANC and the Communist Party had been involved in a whole range of world affairs – like the Peace Council set up by the Soviet Union, and the World Youth Congresses.

The PAC came with a very basic approach: 'You guys know the smallest details about Stalin; you know about other struggles, but don't know the same about African leaders.' The question was coming up again, 'Does Africa not have great thinkers and leaders?' They spoke a lot about this. 'You can tell us all in detail about these great foreign leaders, but what about ours?' They taught that there is only one human race. For the PAC, the thing was that Africans must be one. There must be one Africa – the United States of Africa. So they put that on the agenda for discussion. Others came with African socialism which was being propagated by Julius Nyerere of Tanzania.

Solomon remembers Harry Gwala as a major influence:

He would speak about a whole range of issues and topics, such as the famous American singer, Paul Robeson; philosophers, or some great Shakespearean actor; about culture, drama, and such like.

Gradually, as prisoners got to know one another, as they united in joint struggles like hunger strikes, so the general cells became places of debate and learning.

On Shakespeare ... and more books

Solomon used his time on the island to read:

I have never read so much in my life. In fact, I stopped reading novels for quite a while after the island. I read every major novel: *War and Peace* by Leo Tolstoy; different novels, all the great novels. The Russian writers, Dostoevsky; the French writer Zola; the American writers – the great Jack London, Howard Fast – we read them all. The one book that stands out is William Shirer's *The Rise and Fall of the Third Reich*. And I will never forget Trotsky's biography by Isaac Deutscher.

There is a story about the biography ... When I registered to study with Unisa, I requested the biography of Trotsky. You could only ask for prescribed books. You couldn't ask for recommended books. This

Jack London's *The Iron Heel* was among the great novels consumed by political prisoners.

guy was called Captain Naude; he was in charge of security. He asked, 'What is this?' – showing me the book. The title was *The Prophet Armed*. I told him it is about Christianity – a book about religious struggles and he immediately allowed the book.

The *Shakespeare* Dennis Brutus left behind on the island was widely used:

I think Shakespeare was important at the time because his writings covered such a wide range of experiences and emotions; and they appealed to and touched on the many experiences the inmates had experienced and were experiencing at that moment in time. And of course, we had the time to read all the different plays and sonnets at our leisure; and I suppose, precisely because his writings covered such a wide range of experiences and aroused such a wide range of emotions, we could read what suited us and fitted in with our moods at any particular time. What made him so accessible to many inmates was that almost any inmate who was studying what was then called standard six and higher had to read him as part of the prescribed reading. So many inmates, to different degrees, had knowledge of his writings. This made wide discussion of his works amongst a broad layer of inmates possible because there were always classes about this or that study subject. But Shakespeare and many others writers were part of general sharing of what we enjoyed about the books, plays and poems we were reading. It is not unimportant that Shakespeare can be quoted to fit almost any situation, so chaps liked to quote him.

Solomon's favourite is Sonnet 106:

When in the chronicle of wasted time

I see descriptions of the fairest wights,

And beauty making beautiful old rhyme

In praise of ladies dead and lovely knights,

Then, in the blazon of sweet beauty's best,

Of hand, of foot, of lip, of eye, of brow,

I see their antique pen would have expressed

Even such beauty as you master now.

So all their praises are but prophecies

Of this our time, all you are prefiguring;

And, for they look'd but with divining eyes,

They had not skill enough your worth to sing:

For we which now behold these present days,

Had eyes to wonder, but lack tongues to praise.

Time, and looking back in history into the present, beauty, the physical and spiritual, all those themes that focused the mind of the incarcerated for Solomon come together in this sonnet.

And from Dennis Brutus's Yeats, the 'poet who during a period of anti-imperialist resistance articulates the experiences, the aspirations, and the restorative vision of a people suffering under the dominion of an offshore power' (Said 1994:266), Solomon marks out the last line from *Easter 1916*: 'A terrible beauty is born'.

The prisoners started a Story Writing Programme and a competition. Solomon won second prize.

Marcus Solomon's second prize was for a 'true-experience' story he wrote. In his story,

a group of guys go to jail and the one guy eventually turns State witness – his reasoning being that he wants to save his family; he must look after his family. They are putting pressure on him – the cops – and they are saying that his family said he must turn State witness. Faced with these challenges, when he gets home, his family rejects him. His children say, 'How can you do this to us? You know the trouble you have caused us, your children, at the schools. People are ostracising us because our father is a State witness.' The wife says, 'How can you do this to me? The community here is ostracising me, because my husband, even before you went to the court to give evidence it was already known that you had become an *impimpi*

[traitor].' Eventually he had to leave that place and his family was devastated – broken up. The irony is that the people he wants to help had to turn against him because they were trying to support him. He loses on both sides.

When I came out they confiscated the prize certificate, which was signed by Steve Tshwete. So, there was a whole context, and eventually a library. We had every possible opportunity to read. I even read the story of *Le Corbusier*, the famous French architect. Oh fantastic. We studied Housing and Economics. We had a copy of Karl Marx's book, *Das Kapital*, but it was covered with the cover of an Afrikaans novel, *Trompie*, by the famous South African writer, Topsy Smith.

Having been imprisoned from 1964 to 1974, Solomon was granted permission to study around 1966. Then, for a year, his studies were taken away for starting a riot in the quarry. Despite this, he obtained his university degree in 1973 from Unisa. He also has an Honours Degree in History which he got when he was on the outside. After his release from prison, having completed his Honours Degree, Solomon never studied further. He had intended to do a Master's at the University of Cape Town at a later date, but decided he was done with studies. He did most of his studying on the island.

As a teacher in prison, Solomon witnessed the progress of those inmates who were working at reading and writing for the first time. It was a learning process for both student and teacher – experiencing people's reactions when they got their certificate, or when they passed Standard 6 or Matric, and got their degrees. Having obtained his own degree while incarcerated, he understood the sense of accomplishment among the prisoners.

The lower you went, guys got Standard 6, and there, the achievement, you sensed it. It was such a big thing for them. The most beautiful experience I had was somebody who said, 'I can now read. I don't have to give my private letters to somebody else to read.' That was always very embarrassing – a chap comes and has a confidant; the old people had their confidants, whom they had trust and confidence in. I had one chap telling me a story – of how his wife is writing to

A reconstruction of the chess pieces made by prisoners.

him in Xhosa about what is happening outside, and somebody else has to read it to him. He'd get a letter from his wife, who tells him, 'my husband, I don't have any more underwear. I am so poor. I walk around without underwear.' The reader was younger and it embarrassed both of them.

During the struggle we had a renaissance ... literature — we had beautiful culture. Chaps were writing music, plays, poetry, novels. The prisoners performed plays, the choir sang and Handel's *Messiah* was rendered at Christmas time.

The future is now

'It's a poor sort of memory that only works backwards,' the Queen remarked.

Lewis Carroll, *Through the Looking Glass*

Solomon spent much of his post-Robben Island life working with young children. There were deeply personal reasons. He had four brothers and four sisters. When his mother died, six of the children were sent to an orphanage. He also was sent to Cape Town and had to live without a family environment. After the island he was also confronted with his daughters growing up.

There were also broader political issues. Solomon and his wife, Theresa, had been part of a study group in the late 1970s in Mitchells Plain. One of the questions they confronted was where priorities should lie in organising anti-capitalist forces.

One of the dominant ways of thinking on this issue was that one should concentrate on the organised working class. For people like Solomon, this focus was too narrow. For him, the working class was not limited to factories and it was just as important to have 'politics' in the home and in the community.

These discussions led to a focus on how children in the home are socialised, what is their worldview, how do they think through issues of 'race' and gender?

They read and debated the issue of an alternative education for liberation. While they had broad ideas about students in high school and university, they found themselves confronted with 'What is alternative education for a five year old?'

We made a conscious decision in that study group to set up our own alternative crèche ... with the idea of not teaching but creating an environment in which children can grow fully, emotionally, collaterally, so that the physical development, sports, exercise, is just as important as the mental, in fact the two can't be separated. So it was out of that discussion we set up the crèche ... out of that group a women's forum developed, a youth study group.

For Solomon, through these endeavours:

the main mission is to build a children's movement ... so for me it is a very important political project. Having children become active participants in creating the environment in which they will grow ... children as co-constructors of their own environment ... people want to teach, and of course let me say, it is the culture that children must listen to adults, the adults must teach, but today which adult is really a good teacher with this alcoholism, the violence, the rape, all very negative influences. So we say children must become partners, they constitute half the country's population, 20 million children and half of those are girl children and the majority of our kids are under 15, so it is a very important constituency and this is where the disaster of our education system is failing us, because we had hoped with the new South Africa there would be a major focus on creating an environment in which children can learn.

Solomon is aware that a number of his former comrades argue that capitalism is a reality, and business interests are too powerful. These former allies now argue that one has to act inside capitalism through programmes like black economic empowerment (BEE). Solomon scoffs at this, saying that these are the very same people who confronted and defeated the 'reality' of apartheid.

For Solomon, the problem is that 'people relied on false gods to lead them to Jerusalem'. The important thing is the belief in people as agents of change, and this includes children.

Our slogan is, if you want to change the world, start with yourself. In fact, our slogan is also 'the future is now', you can't wait, because a lot of people say children are the future. We challenge that, in fact we reject it. Children are not the future just like that, they are now. The future is now.

**Prison number: 148/63.
Sizakele Thomson Gazo**, a member of the Pan-Africanist Congress of Azania.

ROBBEN ISLAND

SIZAKELE THOMSON GAZO

Fighting in the present, learning for the future

By getting that education (on Robben Island), we were actually learning, ourselves, for the future, not for the present. For the present, it was fight until the end.

Sizakele Thomson Gazo (interview)

Sizakele Thomson Gazo[17] spent 15 years on Robben Island from 1963 to 1978:

> I was staying in Cape Town with my father and I was arrested in 1961 for public violence. I was discharged in November 1962. But then, in December, I was arrested in Beaufort West and tried for sabotage in Queenstown in March. I was sentenced on April 4th 1963 to Robben Island where I spent my whole fifteen years.

Gazo's arrest was precipitated by his group planning to foster rebellion in the Transkei.

> In December 1962 I was among a group of militant activists who left Langa in Cape Town for Transkei to start the armed revolution of the PAC and the feared Poqo [the PAC's armed wing, which later became the Azanian People's Liberation Army – Apla] of the time. Unfortunately our group was ambushed in a moving train at Beaufort West by the apartheid regime's army and police. One other group was also ambushed at the Queenstown station but fought back bravely. A third group, which was the first to leave Cape Town succeeded in reaching Cofimvaba in Transkei, but due to informers, they were also ambushed at the Ntlonze Mountains.

> My group of seventeen were arrested and sent to Cofimvaba first and then to Queenstown as awaiting trial prisoners. On the 8 April 1963, four were acquitted as they were found with no weapons during our arrest and the rest including me were found guilty of sabotage and sentenced to fifteen years on Robben Island Prison.

The desire of Gazo's group to reach the Transkei and foment rebellion was one of a number of examples of concentrated activity by Poqo, the armed wing of the PAC, in the area. Historian Tom Lodge, for example, writes that by the end of 1962 there were 'three attempts on (Chief) Mantanzima's life. All were Poqo inspired' (Lodge 1985:287).

Borrowing from Julius Caesar, this phenomenon was immortalised by *Drum* magazine's writer, Can Themba:

> Apparently, Chief Kaiser Msi had trampled down the haughty head of most of the lesser chiefs in the Transkei ... He was so widely acclaimed

by the rabble and the world at large that many of the disgruntled chieftains murmured: 'Why, man, he doth bestride the narrow world/ Like a Colossus.' But there were other Xhosas, mostly from the cities who resented the rise of this upstart. A bright idea hit them! What they needed was a high-placed Xhosa ... Dilizintaba Sakwe. As the Americans would say, they sold him the line of how Kaiser was ambitious, and his ambitions threatened the weal of the Transkei, and how Kaiser had to die that Transkei might live ... On Ntsikana's Day ... the conspirators approached (Kaiser) ... they stabbed him, one after another, and when he saw Sakwe also as one of his killers, he cried out in anguish: 'Tixo nawe, mntwanenkosi!' (God you are my son!) ... Ah, me ... that is fantasy. (Themba, quoted in Distiller 2005:174–175)

Themba's article written in 1963 was not the stuff of fantasy. By this time, people like Gazo, 'Xhosas mostly from the cities', were already on their way to Robben Island, guilty of plotting the fall of their 'fellow tribal' leader.

Alice

Gazo was born on 5 August 1939 in the Elangeni Location of Alice. In 1946 he began attending the Lovedale Primary School.

> I passed Standard Six in December 1953 and proceeded to the Lovedale High School in January 1954. When I was completing my Junior Certificate in 1956, I became involved in mischievous activities which resulted in me being arrested with my friends, Jake Nduluka, Qebeyi Nondzube, Oupa Bomi and Taxman Nduluka. After being found guilty we were all given six lashes and discharged. This also resulted in me being expelled from the school in August 1956.

> Because I disappointed my parents, I decided to run away and left for King William's Town, not knowing what I was going to do there. Interestingly I met two guys who were also wandering about like myself and we became friends just after a few chats. They were known as Stax and Sdakana, both of Tshatshu Village in King William's Town. We then decided to join a recruitment agency which was to take us to the Sugar refineries in Durban on a contract basis. To our surprise we were taken to the sugar plantations – a place similar to

a prison if not a slave camp in those days. We stayed there for only three weeks and we were arrested for inciting others not to work under such appalling conditions. After being warned at the charge office, we were taken back to the same farm. We then decided to fake illness so that we were not sent to the fields. You will not believe me when I tell you that there were only two medicines for any type of illness, one for stomach cleaning and the other for rubbing body pains. We were left with no choice but to run away from the place on foot as we had no money for transport.

> We left for home leaving Durban on a Sunday afternoon. We could only afford a half-a-loaf of bread with water a day as I was the only one with a few pounds. We bought a guitar which Stax played on the way but also brought trouble for us, as on the way some boys wanted to take it by force and we had to fight for it. We walked day and night for eleven days; I need not relate every detail of that journey – all I can say is that it was an experience I will never forget ... we reached Mount Frere in Transkei. On the eleventh day, we decided to go to another recruitment agency, Teba, for the Transvaal gold mines. We were sent to the Daggafontein mines in Springs for a six-month contract.

> As I was better educated I got a better job of being an underground checker but my friends unfortunately had to be diggers of gold. They left after completing their contract but I remained behind. I then moved from Springs to Boksburg and finally to Germiston mines ... homesickness compelled me to leave that happiness and in July 1959 I left for home. My parents, brothers and sisters were all so overjoyed to see me back unharmed.

But soon Gazo was on the move again. 'When I became a man, I left for Cape Town. That was in August 1959.'

In February 1960, Gazo went to hear Robert Sobukwe and other PAC leaders speak. As the general secretary of the PAC in the Western Cape, Phillip Kgosana remembers:

> Sobukwe addressed us at Bhunga Square, where we talked about *abelungu abasithandayo* (a searing reference to white people who profess affection for black people while exploiting them

64

for commercial gain). He explained to ordinary workers from EmaMpodweni (Pondoland) and they understood him. He talked well, with his mastery of Xhosa, his mother tongue. (Kgosana, quoted in SADET 2008:152)

Gazo was one of those mesmerised: 'When I heard what they had to say, I responded to myself: "Why can't I join? I am a youth." Then I jumped the wagon.'

Gazo was part of the famous march that planned to go to Parliament in Cape Town in March 1960. This was the march that wrote the PAC's Phillip Kgosana into the history books:

> The march itself … We did go to Cape Town and those were difficult circumstances. Luckily, because we were not violent, they didn't shoot us there. They only shot us when we were at Langa because they came there to disperse the gathering which Kgosana was actually addressing at the Langa Cape Flats. That is where the shooting started. Many people were killed there. I am not really sure of the figure. You know, there are those which could not be accounted for.

The march was supposed to go to parliament. As the march gathered thousands and reached the outskirts of the city, Kgosana was persuaded to attend a meeting at Buitenkant police station.

After the meeting, Kgosana called off the march to parliament after he was promised a meeting with the Minister of Justice, F C Erasmus. The meeting never took place. Instead, when they went to meet the Minister, Kgosana and other members of the delegation were arrested.

Poqo – made in Africa

> Poqo is the pure Africans. Poqo, we are pure Africans. We are not mixed. We are not coming from America. We are not coming from Europe. You were born and bred here in Africa. You don't have any other roots except here in Africa.

This is what Poqo meant for Gazo. Poqo is 'a shortened version of the Xhosa name for PAC, *UmAfrika Poqo*, or "Africans alone", ie, no Europeans'

(Gerhart 1978:225). What distinguished Poqo was that it 'was the first African political movement in South Africa to adopt a strategy that explicitly involved killing people and it was probably the largest active clandestine organisation of the 1960s' (Lodge 1985:241).

Gazo was part of the first group of Poqo soldiers who were tried in the High Court in Queenstown. He cannot remember his name, but Gazo says the judge was a very brutal judge. 'It was a white guy. Don't forget that we had to defend ourselves, and where there were so many questions you couldn't even ask. They say, "No, that is for your lawyer, not for you." That is the type of hearing we had to undergo. No lawyer.'

After he was sentenced, Gazo was taken to Robben Island. Gazo, and with a wry smile, still remembers the trip on the ferry to the island:

> It was bad because I had a problem. When I get into a car, immediately I sense that smell … I will vomit in a car. So when I went in that water … It was not very long, and then I started vomiting until I reached the shore on the other side.

Cell C1

> My ambition on the island was to study. So I was sent to cell C1, which was called the University of Makana. This cell was for those who were granted permission to study … The craving for education was intense. In other cells learning – using the cement as paper – was undertaken by those who were semi-literate, and those who left school at an elementary level. Those who were better educated helped those who were not. The aim was to wipe out illiteracy among us, and build a step to higher education. (Zwelonke 1989:15)

Those who wanted to study were confronted with the problem of money. In addition to many not having access to funds, those family members who supported them were

> being roughed-up outside, and being told not to interact with your people in Robben Island, very few of our people outside would even take that risk of ensuring that you get that money in prison so that you can educate yourself. It was not easy. Fortunately for me, my sister

was brave enough to say, 'No man, I am going to organise funds for my brother', and we were actually being helped by the [International] Defence and Aid Fund in London, so they would channel the funds through your relatives who had the same surname as you. Otherwise, if they had a different surname, they will not accept that money. If to Gazo, a Gazo must send that money, and they will probably monitor that Gazo to see how little he or she is to you and, if possible, they will harass that person so that they decide to not continue with that assistance, so that I cannot further my education.

When Gazo lived in Alice, during his youth, he did not complete his Matric. He made it as far as Standard 9. He completed Matric on the island. 'That was in 1978. I started my degree in 1979. I completed it on the outside.'

Sitting with a Matric Certificate on Robben Island, Gazo's thoughts were still on the defeat of apartheid.

> All my worries were that I must be free – that is all. That is what my test was. The education, of course, we were kidding ourselves. When we are free, we can be able to use those skills and achievements. I didn't expect to use them during the apartheid regime because I didn't know whether I am going to learn when I go outside. Life was not easy. I could have been killed. That is the thing. So, by getting that education, we were actually learning ourselves for the future, not for the present. For the present, it was fight until the end.

Through Unisa, Gazo started studying for a degree and lectures took on the most unusual of forms:

> You know what we were doing? When we were at the quarry we had some groups ... Sedick Isaacs – he was actually teaching me mathematics up to Matric. So, while he was teaching me up to Matric, I was also teaching mathematics to the junior ones. That is what we did to assist each other. When we were in the cells, normally by eight o' clock you must sleep, and these guys would check on you. Although they wouldn't open the door, they would just look and peep through the windows to see whether the people are sleeping. So what I would do, I would actually use my blanket and my clothes to make as if I was in the bed sleeping. They peep in the windows and they would see everybody ... all sleeping. But, at that time, I was

busy doing my assignments ... you would take that risk because you wanted to be sure that you pass.

One of the things that stands out for Gazo was the way prisoners engaged one another about things that they were learning and shared knowledge with those who came to the island with very little experience of formal schooling:

> Some of our people ... came from the Transkei. These people couldn't even read or write, but I am telling you, many of them when they came out, they could read and they could write – I mean, up to Standard 6 level ... Because we taught them; not the system ... We taught them ourselves, in those groups there in the cells.

The prisoners had their own system.

> It was normal in the sense that you had committees. So, even with those study groups, we would have a committee which sort of acted as educators or whatever you call it. Those other people, to have those certificates, they prepared for you ... Just to say that I got something, I have achieved something, I have passed, and so I am going to the next level. But what is important is that when opportunities arise, that person won't have to start from scratch. I mean that people who came to Robben Island without knowing how to read, if you go outside now, people can assure you it was easy for them to go and get their higher certificates. I can say I know who is in Robben Island, and who didn't know how to write or to read, and who today now has a formally recognised certificate. With that knowledge they got from Robben Island, surely it made moving on easier.

Political science

Different political organisations formed committees that provided political education.

> I won't talk about others. I will talk about mine. We were having those groupings. It was during the evening. Actually before you do the study work, you share your political knowledge. Some of us came to Robben Island when we had a far advanced understanding of our organisations. Then there were others who were caught before they

were actually involved in the organisation. But because anything, which the white regime would regard as being challenged, they would pin it on political organisations – PAC or ANC – even if you are not a member. So some of our people were arrested because they were suspected of aiding or abetting these movements. And, unfortunately, the justice system worked hand in hand with the regime so they would simply put you behind bars, and then from there you were found guilty, and you were sent to Robben Island. So, we had to make sure that those are the people that must have the political knowledge so that they become fully fledged freedom fighters. It was like a competition because the ANC would try and move those people towards them so that they could become fully fledged ANC members, and we would do the same thing for the other side.

Gazo remembers debates that were had over the influence of imperialist powers in Africa, communism and one he particularly recalls with a wry smile, over tobacco:

Should tobacco be destroyed? Some felt that smoking should be stopped especially since it came from Rhodesia. I defended the growing and smoking of tobacco because I was a heavy smoker.

There were limits though:

What we tried to avoid – because we didn't want it – was a situation where the whites would see us fighting against each other. We respected each other politically, so we would not entertain that – where you would have PAC and ANC fighting and arguing. We wouldn't have such political debates against each other. We didn't do that. When we are together you deal with common issues. For instance, we were playing rugby together ... so in such areas we didn't see ourselves as being ANC or as PAC. We were just together and that helped a lot. It actually improved our relationship in prison and even outside – we still have that spirit of togetherness ... an ANC member and a PAC member.

There were valuable lessons that Gazo carried with him when he left Robben Island:

What I can say is that I have learnt [from Robben Island], first of all, to be realistic in whatever you do.

And be prepared to face any odds during your lifetime. Things are not as easy as you might imagine. That is what I have learnt because, if you have decided on a course of action and you are sure that it is the right one, be determined to fulfil it. Don't be sidetracked by

Thomson Gazo started his Bachelor of Commerce degree on the island. He completed it after his release.

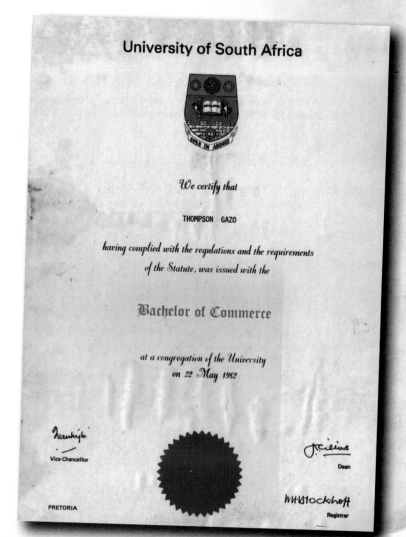

events. Focus on what you believe is your goal and don't go change it. Otherwise, if I didn't have that in mind, I wouldn't be a graduate now. I would have said this is not good for me because there were too many interruptions.

And, also learn to accommodate other views. If we didn't have that togetherness, we would not have survived Robben Island. If I am together with Robben islanders, we see ourselves as brothers. We don't see ourselves as being former people of PAC or ANC or whatever. We learnt that in prison.

The assistance of fellow prisoner Sedick Isaacs was of great value to Gazo.

He was very good. I mean, he was like an ordinary teacher, but he was very strict – a very strict guy. He was very involved in his books. All the time he was reading books. That is what that guy was doing. But if you need assistance from him you will get it. He was very, very good. I am good in mathematics because of him. Even during exams, I don't remember him getting anything less than a B or either an A in his subjects – he was very clever.

Releasing Robben Island

I never wished to talk about the island. I did not talk about it even to my family. It was a strain for me to even think of talking about it. I always felt as if I was crowded into a corner by a ghost, a vicious monster I could not see, holding me spellbound. And when a man asked about the place, I would feel exasperated ... I would give terse answers and never explain anything, and my questioner would give up. (Zwelonke 1989:1)

Like Zwelonke, Gazo is at first reluctant to talk about the adversity and suffering on the island. 'I don't want to talk about. You know, these guys, maybe they want to talk about the hardship – the hardship we got there.'

And then like Zwelonke, 'the closed book' opens (Zwelonke 1989:30). Just a little.

You were mixed with criminals ... and the warders were ruthless – very, very ruthless – because these guys, in the morning when you wake up very early, and they take you outside there in the open field, they give you that sort of porridge. After that ... you have to undress, naked. You stand there. You are waiting for the shacks there –where you go in, and you take clothes, and then you go to the quad. When you come back, at around about four o' clock, you must undress again. You wear other clothes, because they were mistaken that we had *muti* [locally grown and prepared medicines], so they didn't trust us. And you wait there – even in the morning, when it is very cold. In April, it is cold. We wait there for fifteen to twenty minutes, just being tortured by these people. So it was a very bad experience. But, because we were so determined, we knew we expected such things to happen – I mean, even death for that matter. You knew anything could happen to you, so it was that spirit that kept us alive.

My life was not good from 1963 to 1965; it was very, very bad. It was only after 1965. There was a guy, Dennis Brutus. I think he was released in either 1964 or early 1965. That is the guy who actually helped us because he managed to skip the country and went to Europe, and he managed to put our stories out. It was only then that the International Red Cross managed to come to Robben Island. It was only then that they realised things are not well. Although the whites tried to threaten us by saying that if we talk to these people they will make life even worse, we knew they were lying. So, we told our stories to the Red Cross and things started to change.

Brutus in fact gave testimony to the United Nations Special Committee on Apartheid in 1967. His testimony was given wide coverage and used in many publications such as the International Defence and Aid Fund (Sisulu 2004:292).

I mean, these *boers* were very cruel. There was a captain there. He was a one-eyed guy. He was a ruthless guy. Uneducated. I don't know where they got these people from, but they were all of the same culture – ruthless and uneducated. All they know is to insult you, kick you and assault also. And they were getting those instructions from the captain. That guy would come. If he comes, you must take off your cap. And, if you didn't they are going to hit you. Hard. You go to the quarry there. I mean, when you talk about the quarry, I don't know if you have seen a quarry. But the quarry today – the ones where you see the machinery and you drill and you see the stone falling. We would do it with hammers and chisels – big chisels and hammers to hit. It was bad. Some of us would use wheelbarrows – wheelbarrows without tyres; wheelbarrows with an iron wheel – which you can't drive. You have to do that because they were going to hit you.

Gazo also talks about prisoners being buried and then beaten especially in 1963 and 64. The most notorious example of this was the beating of Johnson Mlambo who was buried with only his head sticking out:

A white warder, who had directed the whole business, urinated into Mlambo's mouth. Then vicious blows of fists and boots rained around the defenceless head sticking out of the ground. He did not cry or speak out. When they were tired of the fun, they left him to help himself out of the grave. (Zwelonke 1989:14).

Living on the outside

When I was released I was taken straight back to Alice, where there was nobody. Nothing. I had been banned from Cape Town. I had to fend for myself. Fortunately, I had a sister Nokhulu in the area, so occasionally I would come to my sister to visit. That is when I just saw a bus moving on the highway and saw an address on the bus. I took that address on the bus and I applied. I was so fortunate I was called for an interview. But then the security guys in Zwelitsha saw my name there. I was told I did not get the employment. But after some time, somehow they managed to get through to them and these guys decided to call me. Actually they wrote me a letter – the security people in Zwelitsha, they wrote me a letter. I was not to be employed anywhere in the Ciskei government. I would not get a position because of my involvement in politics. So, I took it as that until we are free. Just understand that.

Fortunately we were still getting financial aid from the international funds, so I managed to be able to buy bread and a few things.

Then Gazo got a call to meet Charles Sebe, security head of the Ciskei and brother of Chief Minister, Lennox Sebe.

His brother was the president, so when I was called there I met him with his 'left hand' – a certain Makhuzi – very, very secure with everything; all types of weapons inside there. What they did first is to boast about these weapons and so on.

And then they asked about me – who I am? I told them. Then, through that discussion, this guy Charles realised that 'this guy has got a potential' and I heard him speak to his brother – that is the president, Lennox. 'He seems to be good. Can't we take him to one of our departments?' I don't know what the brother said, but then he came to me, and they wanted to take me.

Gazo was circumspect:

I must be clever here. I didn't want to obviously say, 'I don't want your position.' I said, 'Well, I applied for a position in another place and then if those people agree to release me, I don't have a problem.' So they said, 'Okay. Well, we will discuss this matter with them.' Unfortunately they did not manage to win those guys. 'We want this man. We don't want anyone else,' they said. And that is when I managed to get a job – on November 1st 1979. I started with that company in Zwelitsha – and I was an assistant accountant. I very quickly became an accountant and I ended up being a senior accountant for that company until 1989 when I left them for another corporation – a government corporation. Then in 1990 they wanted to start a new operation and they took me as the chief executive officer of Mayibuye Bus Company until I retired in 2003. So I am a retired person.

After the unbanning of the PAC, Gazo became involved officially with the organisation. In 1997 he withdrew from political involvement for reasons he is not prepared to discuss. Today Gazo works for his church – a branch of the Presbyterian Church, started by a Reverend Ntiyosoka in Port Elizabeth – called Old Memoriam:

I am a church boy now. I am involved in church activities throughout. When I wake up I do church work, even now. If you didn't come now, I would be on my computer doing church work. I am not interested in contemporary politics. I think I have done my part of the struggle. I am very happy.

Prison number: 376/64. Monde Colin Mkunqwana, a member of the ANC and Umkhonto we Sizwe. He remembers reading *Richard III* on Robben Island, and eventually came to play the role of Richard III.

Monde Mkunqwana sat for his senior certificate (Standard 10) exams while on Robben Island in 1974.

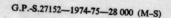

G.P.-S.27152—1974-75—28 000 (M–S)

BO/BE 325

DEPARTEMENT VAN BANTOE-ONDERWYS
DEPARTMENT OF BANTU EDUCATION

TOELATINGSKAART EN EKSAMENROOSTER
ADMISSION CARD AND EXAMINATION TIME-TABLE

SENIORSERTIFIKAATEKSAMENS,
SENIOR CERTIFICATE EXAMINATIONS,
NOVEMBER 1974

Naam van kandidaat/Candidate's name

Mkunqwana Colin Monde

Persoonsnommer/Identity number

Eksamennommer
Examination number

Hierdie nommer moet op die antwoordeboek ingevul word

N° 23051

This number must be written on the answer book

MONDE COLIN MKUNQWANA

'Opening the world through education'

I remember we had in our trial Comrade Mgabela. He couldn't read or write. When we got to the island Mgabela was one of my students – teaching him, I think, Standard 2 or 3 up to Standard 6. He passed Standard 6. Then his certificate was sent to him by the Education Department. You could see that when he received that certificate there was an atmosphere of happiness – starting with him. You could see his face smiling immediately when he got that certificate. We used to stay in one cell. Then the whole cell burst into happiness, which is a manifestation of a realisation – the effect and the years of toil, and the mark of success in his life. He never thought that he would get a certificate in his life, Comrade Mgabela.

What's in a name?

Monde Colin Mkunqwana[18] was born in Selborne in East London on 20th April 1939. 'I share the same birthday with Adolf Hitler.' During that time, Selborne was a suburban area reserved for whites. Mkunqwana's parents worked for the Georges, a middle class family who ran a medium-size business in East London.

As the Group Areas Act began to take effect in the mid-1950s, Mkunqwana's parents had to move to a township not far from Selborne. That was the turning point in his life – taken from living in a white area with all the facilities to a black township which had

> no facilities and hills of rubbish. I had attended the United Higher Primary School which was under a very famous man called Dickson Dyani – it was amongst the first African schools in East London. Then I proceeded from primary school to Welsh High School where I got involved politically. That was about 1958. The conditions in the township really intensified my conviction now to join an organisation which would change the living conditions of the African people for the better. I had lived in an area called Gomoro which was a shanty town. Gomoro was one of the parts of the Eastern Location where there was a lot of gambling and prostitution, and a lot of violence. Now under those conditions people get conscious of what is going on – comparing with the white settlement in the other side of the city.

Mkunqwana is very proud of his English name, Colin, even though he understands the 'historical background' that 'an African who was born in an English colony where all Africans must have Christian names, that is

English, which means that we had been transformed from what we were to what we are'.

For Mkunqwana, rather 'it is a question of being proud of the people who gave me this name'. The people who named Mkunqwana Colin were his parents' employers, the George family, whom he describes as being 'very much supportive' of his parents during his incarceration on Robben Island. In fact, the first batch of money which he used to pay for his studies [Matric] on the island came from them.

When he was growing up they would encourage Mkunqwana to further his studies and get an education. They ran a bottling company in East London called East London Bottling, popularly known as Coca-Cola, where Mkunqwana's father used to work. During the school holidays, Monde would also be called in to work. As a result, he never had problems with pocket money throughout his school life.

Then, Mkunqwana was arrested and charged with sabotage.

While sitting as an awaiting trial prisoner in December 1963, Mkunqwana was shocked when the George family visited him in East London Prison.

> They brought me some Christmas presents and chicken, and everything that you can think of – so you know what the Colin relationship is. Even now, if I go to Cape Town, I see Mrs George there, who is a wife of one of the sons. If I go to Jo'burg, there are also Georges. We were always together. They even visited my house when I was still there in Beacon Bay. I even communicate with the other Georges around the country, so I am part of their family really. So, I can't say why I should reject 'Colin' when I have such good relationships with these people. I am very proud of my name because of these facts.

Around the same time that Mkunqwana was attempting to improve the living conditions of his community, the ANC was debating the shift towards armed struggle. Monde was drawn to Umkhonto we Sizwe.

Entering the ANC

Mkunqwana remembers clearly his induction as a young person into the ANC and subsequently into MK:

> The youth were initiated into the ANC by older men. That meant getting involved, getting to know the policies of the organisation, how it works, how they operate, and being instilled with firm discipline. For instance there was what was called 'volunteer oath'. That volunteer oath was a guide for your discipline, how you relate with people, how you relate with the organisation, and loyalty. That becomes very important – the respect that you give to the organisation and your leaders. That would really form a fundamental foundation for you as a member. There would be public meetings and then branch meetings and, it is like any organisation – you can't attend a branch meeting without being initiated – just like a church. Then later on, after the establishment of MK, you were selected and recruited from the ANC into Umkhonto.

This recruitment meant avoiding ANC activities, including attendance of branch meetings. 'We would get a political commissar and they would come from all over – Johannesburg, especially from PE [Port Elizabeth] and then locally.'

With the recruitment into MK, a new induction began:

> We started at a very elementary level with elementary methods. We were not military trained, you know. We were not trained in explosives – it was a question of trial and error – but, the army that we formed grew up and we had to draw some targets. Targets were Government buildings, collaborators in the township, collaborators with the Government and we were very active. We shook the whole of East London, King William's Town, and the whole of the border area. Now that is, as I said, the activities of MK.

The road to Robben Island prison

Mkunqwana's commander was Washington Mpumelelo Bongo, who was executed in 1964. This came in the wake of the hanging of three Eastern

Cape MK soldiers, Vuyisile Mini, Wilson Khayingo and Zinakile Mkaba on 6 November 1964. They were the first MK soldiers to be executed.

> We were saved – I don't know whether by age, 24 years, or by a stroke of luck, or by God's grace. There were three of us who were supposed to have gone with those men – Zola Mjo, Fezile Mlanda – and myself. I think the judge was sober enough to realise that we were not supposed to hang. I was sentenced to 22 years – 8 years concurrently, and so effectively 14 years. Zola Mjo was effectively [given] 20 years, but he was sentenced to a total 35 years. Likewise with Fezile Mlanda – he got 47 years, but served 23 years.

The trial was conducted in Queenstown in 1964. It ran from February to March 1964. Then Mkunqwana was transferred back to East London from Queenstown, and from East London to Port Elizabeth – each prisoner handcuffed and chained to another prisoner. When the prisoners got to the town of George en route to Robben Island, they slept over, with ankle manacles on.

> You slept with them, so if I want to go to the loo, I have to wake up the other prisoner. Then, if my stomach runs, that is unfortunate – I have to wake him up. While he is doing it, I am standing there because we cannot get separated.

The group arrived on the island on 9 April 1964:

> There were two days of admission. It was hell. We were admitted into the old jail – the offices were still there, but the prison population was already huge. It was a huge jail. Early in the morning there was still the zinc *tronk* [jail] – we slept there. In the morning, how they beat us. They would open all doors, and then lock the main grill which leads out into the other cells of the prison. They would come like flies on us with batons and they would hit us. After they had beaten us, we were collected and assembled, and then the jailer, Bantjie Theron, that chap was very cruel. Of all the people that I have met, he was the cruellest guy. Theron – taking advantage of people who are defenceless, and then instigating other warders to assault us. That carried on for almost 48 hours. And they would even instigate criminals to assault us, and if you dare fight with a criminal, well, that is an offence already. You get punished for that, in spite of the fact

that the criminal had assaulted you first, and you are retaliating. This carried on for some years, until I think up to 1967.

Cementing learning

'When you learn to read you will be born again … and you will never be quite so alone again' – Rumer Godden.

During the apartheid era, a Standard 8 (Grade 10) qualification was referred to as a Junior Certificate (JC). For most people of colour, reaching this level of education was considered a great achievement – those who had one carried it with pride and honour. Mkunqwana made it as far as Standard 8 at Welsh High School.

> Now when I got into prison, the influence of those comrades who were more educated than us, like Fikile Bam, Neville Alexander, and also the influence of our Rivonia Trial comrades. Mandela, Comrade Kathy [Kathrada], Walter Sisulu, emphasised the importance of education and the eradication of illiteracy – not only on Robben Island, but in the country.

According to Mkunqwana, the average level of education among the inmates was Standard 1. But there were also teachers, those with high school education and with degrees in the general section.

> Our leadership had to attend to this because we were serving long sentences and people had to sit down and learn. And those who could teach others had to roll up their sleeves. This was done without the intervention of the authorities. Then we started dividing and categorising ourselves – from Sub A, right up to Standard 2, and then onwards: Standards 3, 4, 5, 6, then JC, and then Matric. It had very good results after some years because I remember I was also hooked in as a teacher. I was not trained as a teacher, but because at least I had JC and those years our JC standard was more powerful than it is now.

> I used to teach Standard 6 and lower. I also used to attend classes myself because I was busy with studying for Matric. Then, after a

period of two or three years, many of the illiterate comrades could read and write their names, and their own letters.

The authorities sought to introduce their own literacy classes 'at a low level of literacy – like Standard 1 and Standard 2'. Alongside this, they tried to destroy the prisoners' own system:

> The authorities realised that there is something going on because they would clean out the cells and search everything. That was the sort of intimidation. And then, during the day, there would be a squad going into the cells to search everything and take every little paper you know, and then destroy those exercise books that we had made out of cement pockets. But we were never deterred. And this had a dividend indeed. I could list a lot of comrades, especially from the Transkei, who now after their release had achieved the standard of Matric. I have met some of them after my release and have come to realise the importance of the education they received in prison.

Mkunqwana entered Robben Island with a JC (Junior Certificate). Thereafter, it took him two years to study for his Matric. His Matric subjects were English, Xhosa, Afrikaans, Mercantile Law, Accountancy and Commerce. He wanted to go for a Bachelor of Commerce, but was unable to as he did not have Mathematics. In prison, Mkunqwana became a teacher, assisting other people to learn how to read and write. Teaching and learning took place in the cells. There was a request that all those from JC (Standard Eight) upwards should teach others. Among the prisoners, a 'national education organisation' was formed, with heads of divisions.

> The very system that you see now, you find with the Department of Education and in schools, principals, and heads of divisions and so on. That was the arrangement of how courses were introduced by those comrades who were teachers from outside so as to systematise our efforts. In our cells, everybody in every cell, who had JC and upwards, was instructed to teach others. It was an interesting situation, honestly. I remember people like Philip Silwana and others who were teachers like Douglas Piti – those were PAC guys, but nevertheless that's the way it would go. It was across the board – we would attend workshops on a Saturday morning on presentation skills. If you did,

> there was a head for commercial studies, who was a teacher – I forget his name. He would take us through the system of presentation and how you solve certain problems with your students. We were really in a university type of atmosphere and one had learnt a lot, as a matter of fact. In fact, I am not a teacher by profession, but where I worked I used to train people. Now they would ask me, 'Man, where did you get all the presentation skills?' And I would say, 'From Robben Island. That is where I learnt, in spite of the fact that I have done some courses in presentation skills here.' Well, that is basically, fundamentally how Robben Island was a school to me.

Uprooted from home, and plunged into a terrifying, unfamiliar environment, Mkunqwana, like many other prisoners, made Robben Island work for him.

Becoming a university

Mkunqwana explains why Robben Island came to be known as the University of Makana.[19]

> This was because all sorts of disciplines would conduct symposiums on certain aspects of international relations, the energy crisis, world crisis in education, and all those challenging issues. And then, witchcraft, of course. Science and witchcraft. So we would have people getting books from the State library, preparing for their presentations. It was an eye opener. Never, at any stage of my life, have I met such an atmosphere. Even outside, while I was studying, none could match Robben Island.

Prisoners were allowed access to books on Robben Island – they were allowed to buy prescribed books according to their studies, and they were also allowed, at a later stage, to become members of the State Library and the Unisa library. But even though some prisoners were not registered for a particular course or subject, they came to benefit:

> Now, you take yourself as being registered for English 1 – instead of sitting and doing nothing, you would go to these lectures on various disciplines by those who had degrees. And, you would study up to Course 3 – and some, even beyond Course 3. By the time you get

registered for Course 1, you are already a graduate. As a result, the pass rate was very high because you are doing standards that you know. Although you are not qualified, but you already have studied this – how to use reference books, how to use prescribed books, how to write an assignment, how to tackle certain questions. Sedick Isaacs, he is a science man. He would take his students to go beyond the matric syllabus. There would be new lecturers, like Marcus Solomon for instance, and he would lecture English. Robben Island had produced the best students. People will get As and Bs.

On Robben Island, there were also some prisoners who were studying technical subjects. John Nkosi and Fezile Mlanda were doing B Compt [Bachelor of Computing]. They were supposed to have a computer, but graduated without one. These stories really inspired prisoners.

According to Mkunqwana, this zealousness to study and the success rate also inspired the warders.

Then the government started to encourage warders to study. They would come for my books on criminology. I had lent this guy – he was a Lieutenant Prins, all my criminology books. He had an assignment and, I am not blowing my trumpet, but I was one of the bright students. So somebody had advised him to 'go to Monde'. Because he had an assignment, that day I did not go to work. We sat down in the cell. I tried to give him some tips and points on how and what to do – I think he got something like 75% – but he never returned my books.

The inmates were not only turning around the environment of brutality, they were developing a culture of learning. This, according to Mkunqwana, was helped by a new head of the prison, John Harding. [20]

He was English, and he was daring, I must say. In fact, he came there to rectify the literacy problem of the warders and we saw a lot of guys being promoted. This guy was a lieutenant. Because he studied criminology, he was doing this.

Captain Marx and Engels

When he was not studying, Mkunqwana devoured anything he could lay his hands on, even *Reader's Digest* stories. The first book that Mkunqwana read in prison was a novel by John Masters called *Bhowani Junction*. The book, published in 1954, was set in India in 1946/7, just as the country was moving to independence. It focused on the Anglo-Indian community. But for Mkunqwana, it also delved into the emergent Cold War, as the

Monde Mkunqwana studied criminology through Unisa.

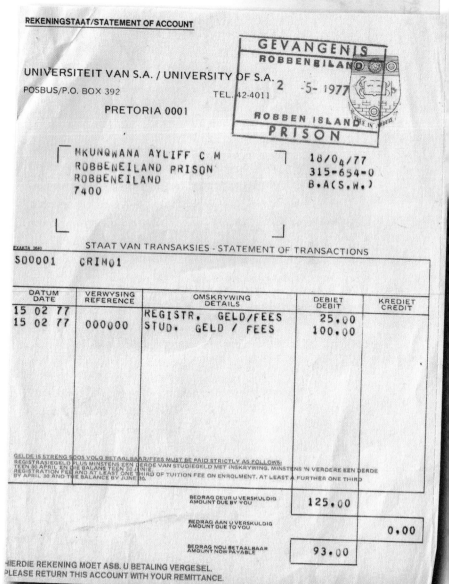

Prisoners could supplement their meagre rations from their allowances.

book illustrated how the British tried to ensure that the communists did not become hegemonic after Indian independence.

He cannot remember where he obtained the book – it was just 'floating around'.

> We used to get some of the most interesting books once we got permission to be State Library members. Then the authorities got wind of some of these books which they would regard as undesirable. They came across Frederick Engels, and then one guy says, 'Wie is Engels, jong? No, this is English. Ag, take your book.' Then they had in their midst a certain warder by the name of Lieutenant or Captain Marx – Captain Marx and Engels – it was just a joke to them. To the rest of us it was not a joke, because we knew Engels and Marx and we knew what they meant to us.

He also explains why it was important for prisoners to be able to read and write.

> From a historical and political perspective, being people who were deprived of basic education – and especially quality education, which is the key to everything – it was important for us. Some of the comrades from Robben Island come to us and say, 'Man, I never thought I would read and write. You have opened the whole world to me.'

Books and the theatre

> I assimilated myself into Cell 1 (C1) like a shooting star dissolving in the darkness of the night. Soon I was taking part in staging a mock trial, and again in staging a mock parliament. C1 was a cooking pot of cultural activity. Our souls were enriched, uplifted from the eroded substratum of basic living. When we staged *Animal Farm*, man, we did not care what military cap peeped through the window. It was enriching the soul. (Zwelonke 1989:69)

Of all the Shakespeare plays that he read on the island, Mkunqwana remembers *Richard III*. One of the reasons for this was he got to play the king on the island in one of their productions. But there were also personal and political reasons: Firstly, there was Richard's deformity and how he refused to let it interfere in his life's ambitions:

> My uncle now, who comes before my mother, was deformed. In fact, I learnt a lot from him. He was a strong man, had a strong character, he was feared, you know, in his village and now that also became an interest to me. I related very well with the character and at the back of my mind was my uncle's character.

Secondly, *Richard III* illustrates contemporary South African life:

> It illustrates the pursuit of power, murder, conspiracy, you know all those which are prevalent today amongst our own people, especially in organisations, and then greed, which was the underlying factor in Richard, hatching all these other plots against his own brothers. While on the island and preparing to play Richard, the most interesting part for me was the plots, you know which we found there. Even then that was in tandem with all the political theories that we learnt and the game of politics: How it is played and how you should position yourself in the leadership.

Mkunqwana remembers reading South African writers, Herman Charles Bosman and Nadine Gordimer. And George Eliot which held important lessons:

George Eliot, a female but with a male name, now that alone you know says a mouthful about the philosophy of the 19th century, how for a woman to get herself recognised in a man's world, she had to transform herself into a man.

Mkunqwana also had access to Xhosa literature and was inspired, and still is, by the work of Mpilo Walter Benson Rubusana, especially *Zemk' iinkomo Magwalandini,* which was published in 1906:

The title of the book meant the land is becoming a desert. It's a euphemism you know ... a call of wake up you cowards, our stock is being stolen. The crux of the work is to get committed, defend your integrity, get back your country, you know that is what it means, because if your cattle are being stolen, cattle are a source of pride, and then they give life to people in general, so if you take now all those resources, especially the cattle, it means you decimate the nation. That is what Rubusana is portraying – the wars of dispossession.

Monde was also involved in the transcribing of books, vital to the ongoing culture of spreading knowledge through the communal cells:

We would get books from the State library and especially those like Engels and Marx, or anything by the communist Maurice Conforth, who made a very powerful distinction between idealism and materialism. All of those books we transcribed. We would get people with understanding of the issue within the book; they should not be like machines. So, if there are 10 chapters, we would get about five guys to do two chapters, then the whole night, probably the whole week, so by the time the due date comes for the book to be returned to the library, it is all transcribed.

Besides playing Richard III, Monde also had another lead role playing Che Guevara:

This reflected now on the relationship between the ANC and the Cuban Revolution, spearheaded by Che and Castro and Raul and many other comrades. I felt that after Che died that he is going to be portrayed by the western world as a villain, therefore there must be something written in the true perspective of Che's character, so that

play is a tribute. Che as a revolutionary, not only for the people but the whole world.

Mkunqwana is still reading, still buying books:

Books that I buy especially are history books, books on intelligence services, drama. I don't buy fiction, I buy non-fiction stuff. And then autobiographies of people, like Francis Bacon, Waldo Emerson, the writer. Recent African writers, Ngugi, Wole Soyinka, Ghanaian playwrights, I admire very much.

Of course, South African literature, both English and Afrikaans. I have got Afrikaans books here at home. Also the history of intelligence, way back during Roman times, Greek times, and then recent history during the World War, the transformation of the CIA and KGB, the role of intelligence in South Africa, and its transformation, the integration of both forces, from apartheid to liberation. So those are the books that I read. One that I have recently read is a book by Ken Flowers, who was the head of CIO [Central Intelligence Organisation] in Rhodesia. He says a lot about their relationship now with Portuguese intelligence, British intelligence, KGB, all those organisations, so this builds my information on understanding how the world works.

Political education

For Mkunqwana, the central components of political education were about dialogues around freedom, equality and justice.

The ANC conducted political lectures like any other organisation. The PAC did it from their perspective. Political lectures would ground us – help an individual member in understanding the meaning of the liberation struggle from a historical perspective, and the meaning of our relationship with other organisations, especially those Left organisations in the world.

You would find the ANC would befriend, especially in the international arena, all those progressive organisations like the Labour Party in Britain. Also, in Italy, the Communist Party and in Australia the Labour Party because some of the Conservative Parties were friends of South Africa you know – the old South Africa – and they would be reluctant to help us. Those are the aspects and the history of the struggle; the history of the ANC. It's also about the importance of the alliance from the 1930s – that is the involvement of the Communist Party with the ANC in 1946, and the alliance between the Indian Congress and the ANC finally in 1955. This was a trail of events which culminated in a mass democratic movement, nationally and internationally.

According to Mkunqwana, they would also discuss the role of the United Nations as a forum, to express political grievances as South Africans and the Afro-Asian bloc. India had been a friend of the ANC as an organisation and this had an impact on how Indians were viewed locally as well as the ANC's position on non-racialism:

> You see most of the Indian comrades taking prominent positions within the South African spectrum, in organisations and in the government. They deserve to be there. They are South Africans. That is why you see coloured people in the government today, because they are South Africans. They have been in the struggle together. Political education makes you understand the tiniest spectra of political systems – it gives strength even if you are alone; you can start an organisation.

> Anywhere else, you can know how to organise people, how to organise your discipline, how to organise your political education, how to organise your political strategies. That is the result of political education.

Freedom and arrested development

Leaving the island and arriving 'home' after 14 years in March 1978 was arresting to Mkunqwana. Painfully and somewhat ironically, he was thwarted in his quest to study:

> I couldn't even attend a church service. At 6 o'clock I had to be at home until the next day at 6 o'clock – which means for almost 12 hours I had to be house-arrested, in a way. I had to report (to the police station) every first Monday of the month. If I failed to do so, I would have to go back to jail. These were the conditions. And then faced with unemployment and with no financial resources, and with only

R50 per month from the Border Council of Churches, it was an uphill struggle. I still had to write my assignments and do my practicals. I was not supposed even to go within 500 metres of a factory. I was supposed to have one visitor at a time at home. This carried on for a while and that really hampered my studies. I could see my academic ambition being shattered because of these conditions. I had to stop studying and find work.

Eventually Mkunqwana secured work:

> I was confined to the homeland of Ciskei. As a result, I ended up working for the Ciskei government in the Department of Manpower. I started with Education, then Justice, and then finally the Department of Manpower was established. I became one of the officers there. But, I had to reconstruct my life. I didn't even have a bed to sleep on or clothing – I didn't have a lot of necessities.

Fort Hare, Unisa and flying

> 'Do you know what reading is like?' Though the boy has many thoughts on the subject, he shrugs his shoulders … 'It's like flying. Reading a book can take you anywhere in the world.' (Connelly 2008:276)

Mkunqwana married. Having Ntombizini in his life was a turning point:

> I got married because one thing that would not confine me would be getting married. I did that and it really paid off. Anyway, I had to change the course of my studies immediately. After two years, in 1980 or so, I started thinking about studying again. I wanted to be a social worker, but I was still banned. I couldn't go into a factory to do practicals. I couldn't go into any social institution like an orphanage, or so on. So, I had to think about new disciplines. Then I enrolled at Fort Hare which had a branch in Zwelitsha. I did political science, public administration and languages – Afrikaans, Xhosa and English. And, there is another interesting course on African Literature which I really appreciated – it is a sort of a discipline which investigates African beliefs, symbols and totems. This course has developed into a degree level. I did one year with Unisa in Public Administration and Advanced Public Administration theories. Further on, I decided to do my MBA [Master's in Business Administration] with Stellenbosch. But, because

of financial problems, I had to abandon it. So that is the story and how this has helped me in education circles. It has really helped me – now, looking back at where I started, in prison. Being recognised by the whole country because I attend some of these conferences which are relevant to my academic qualifications, I am very humble to say that the influence which our leaders have given me is paying off. Also, as a sideline, I've now started getting into learning to fly.

His interest in flying began at a very early age when one of the older George children built him a model plane, which he flew in the Selborne College grounds. He has collected literature on flying but knows time and age are against his gaining a private pilot's licence. But Mkunqwana is encouraged by the opportunities that post-apartheid South Africa provides for young black people:

Monde Mkunqwana with his family after his graduation from Fort Hare University.

After completing his matric on Robben Island, and studying courses in criminology through Unisa, Monde Mkunqwana eventually graduated with a BA from Fort Hare University after his release from the island.

79

UNIVERSITY OF FORT HARE

DEGREE
OF
BACHELOR OF ARTS

THIS IS TO CERTIFY THAT

MONDE COLIN MKUNQWANA-AYLIFF

WAS THIS DAY AT A CONGREGATION OF THE UNIVERSITY AWARDED THE DEGREE OF

BACHELOR OF ARTS

VICE-CHANCELLOR

DEAN

23 JUNE 1990
DATE

REGISTRAR (Academic)

Now, when I look at these black, you know, young boys, who take up, you know, flying, as a profession, I feel very much elated, as if it is me that is qualified. The sky is the limit really now for all our youngsters, as a matter of fact I am orientating my grandson that one day he should be, you know, a pilot and he is gradually, you know, getting into the spirit. When he sees an aeroplane flying over he says, 'Hey grandpa one day I will fly that one'.

Having devoted his life to learning and political leadership, Mkunqwana, now with thoughts of easing into a cockpit, is 72 years old.

For Mkunqwana:

Reading and writing is a key to one's success in life. Even if you are not that well educated, at least it gives you some semblance of freedom – you do not depend on any individual – and, that is another point. It opens doors for you as it has done now with many comrades all over South Africa today. Even internationally, some are businessmen, some are politicians, some are small enterprises people, some are working and some are successfully retired. So that is the story. That is how it was. Had it not been for Robben Island, I must say, I probably would not have achieved what I have achieved in terms of education. In these national forums I stand tall because I do my research. If, for instance, there is a topic to be discussed, I go to the library and research before, so that I can be confident. My philosophy is to contribute now to the discussions which will culminate in public policy.

80

some mask has fallen, the ma

free, uncircumscribed, but

unclassed, tribeless, And n

from awe, worship, degree, the

imself; just, gentle, wise; l

et free from Gui

This is to certify that

in the year 1971

SEDICK ISAACS

obtained the Degree of

BACHELOR OF ARTS

having satisfied the requirements for the degree in respect of the undermentioned subjects:

MAJOR SUBJECTS

THREE COURSES IN EACH OF : PSYCHOLOGY
MATHEMATICS

SUBSIDIARY SUBJECTS

ONE COURSE IN EACH OF : PHYSICS
ECONOMICS
GEOGRAPHY
PRACTICAL ENGLISH
GERMAN (SPECIAL COURSE)

Ivanhijk

Vice-Chancellor

Dean

B. F. g. van Rensburg

Registrar

PRETORIA, 20 MAY, 1972

Exemption was granted from the following course(s) passed at another university:
PSYCHOLOGY ONE, MATHEMATICS ONE & TWO, PHYSICS ONE.

Prison number: 883/64. Sedick Isaacs was rooted in science and mathematics, and with his voracious appetite for reading and teaching, Isaacs loomed large in the educational inspiration of political prisoners.

SEDICK ISAACS

'A beautiful mind'

'Like the peregrinators of old we exchanged and shared knowledge and ideas whilst pushing wheelbarrows up and down the dykes of the quarry' (Isaacs 2010:188).

Talk to prisoners in the general section of Robben Island and one of the names that inevitably comes up is that of Sedick Isaacs. He had a reputation as a mathematics teacher and general science boffin.

Sedick Isaacs[21] was born in Cape Town and went to Trafalgar High School. Some of the teachers were members of the Non-European Unity Movement and through them Isaacs was exposed to political literature, such as readings on the Algerian revolution.

> But while I did some pamphleteering for the Unity Movement and went to their meetings, it was almost a sense of impotence that, at these meetings, people would come and explain the problems which we had; there were no real practical solutions. I think I am a practical person and therefore moved towards practical politics. It was fairly easy.

Isaacs was caught up in the mobilisation for the anti-pass campaign of the PAC in Cape Town.

The Pan Africanists had just slipped away from the African National Congress in '59 [1959] and they were more energetic, more radical. And I was also energetic and radical, and I thought that would be a good organisation for me. I got very involved with it at the time. (Isaacs, quoted in Wieder 2008:84)

Isaacs was studying at the University of Cape Town:

> My father was a fisherman, but he died when I was six years old and my mother cared and looked after us. My eldest brother went to work at the age of 16 in the building trade. He gave me and my other brother a chance to complete our Matric. Then I got a scholarship at the University of Cape Town. I completed a Bachelor of Science degree with majors in chemistry – the knowledge of which became of huge value to me, because the next phase was more active forms of demonstration – the knowledge of explosives was also useful.

It was the making of explosives that led to his trial for sabotage.

> I got caught doing that. We went to the rural areas to test it. We were driving back and one of my friends stopped, and just when he stopped the police picked us up. I think they were watching. I had a girlfriend who was white. The police were also watching me in terms

of the Immorality Act. And I think that's partly why they might have been watching. (Isaacs, quoted in Wieder 2008:84)

Sedick's trial lasted barely two months. He was sentenced to 12 years on Robben Island and served his time between December 1964 and September 1977. He had nine months added to his sentence when he was caught with a homemade key and a radio on the island.

The brutality

The Security Police with their electric generators, their rubber batons for damaging internal organs of the abdomen and their brutality were after information. Here the brutality was an end in itself. Time seemed to stand still as the torture went on relentlessly with the whole of my body begging to get out of the straps and away from the source of pain. Even though my ankles and wrists were released from the frame, I could not get off immediately. I had to wait for the shriek in my nervous system to subside. Walking unsteadily back to recover my clothing, I remembered briefly hovering on the brink of fainting but with effort I managed to pull myself together and kept my head up. The injuries healed years ago but the psychological effect persists. (Isaacs 2010:144)

Isaacs recounts one of the many brutal punishments he suffered on the island at the hands of warders. Regularly 'singled out and derided as an "amper baas" (almost boss or almost white)', Isaacs presents an 'insider' story of Robben Island from the general section of the prison (Isaacs 2010:10).

His incarceration was trespassed with persistent run-ins with the authorities and he was one of the few prisoners to have his sentence increased on the island for prison offences. The trials for these additional offences were held on Robben Island. He was charged with possession of an implement that could facilitate escape, namely a key and a radio.

Isaacs played a vital part in the making of the key:

I did the initial measurement of the key. I specified the blade size and the barrel size and, when it came from the blacksmith, Jafta

Masemola,[22] I did some further tests on it. I put it in a fire until it became sooty and managed to get the resins off. And I made further specifications to the blacksmith and he filed it that way. The key came in for testing and we managed to open the cell but it was a bit tight and therefore Masemola polished the key to make it a bit more smooth and put oil on it. Then it came in for a second testing. But during that time a radio also came in for repairs (stolen from a warder and smuggled in by common law prisoners) and I was sitting with the radio. Of course, not everybody knows that. It was like on a need-to-know basis so as to not involve others. I didn't know that the radio was missing and they were desperately searching for it all over the place. That was the primary purpose of the search they conducted. Unfortunately they found the radio and the key with me.

He was beaten, chained and thrown into solitary confinement.

In the early years food was 'porridge with the distinctly musty taste and the occasional pinkish streaks – the carcass of worms or maggots that once lived in maize meal before it was cooked to death and served as porridge' (Isaacs 2010:62).

There were also issues around medical care:

Our medical care was very rudimentary. Some of our comrades who saw the doctor, who had prescriptions for medicine or drugs, were stopped after the first two days, saying that we are wasting their government's resources. There was a whole lot of problems and, as prisoners, the only thing we could do was to go on a hunger strike and that was our first hunger strike – not very successful – but it was a start. And I had the bright idea that the hunger strike in prison needs to be published in the newspapers and I wrote the article on what prison conditions were like. At the same time I was also ambitious. I drew a map showing the weak points of the island and where the power supply is and how to possibly disable the power supply as well as the electricity supply, and that led to my first solitary confinement. That lasted almost a year. In fact, I am not quite sure whether it lasted ten months, eleven months, or a year, but I think it was probably just about eleven months.

While the maximum stay in the *culukoet* (the punishment section) was 21 days, Isaacs was to remain in solitary for almost a year. As days turned into weeks and into months, Isaacs tried to ensure he did not 'crack'. Crack was the word used to describe prisoners going through a period of depression, meaning literally

> breaking up, but the tone of the word gradually changed meaning, so that when I announced I was cracking I would mean 'have a little patience with me, I am not myself today'. It was during this period that the pain of imprisonment became worst. Whenever this happened we knew that there would be support in some form, sometimes with encouragement, a bit of humour or just quiet non-verbal support and togetherness. The trick was to sense the type of support that would fit the person 'cracking' and the mood of the moment. (Isaacs 2010:101)

Isaacs did not have this support and tenderness in solitary confinement. He survived by trying to bring some order to his day. For example, every afternoon he 'began doing a bit of mathematics by building equations, deriving their properties and then trying to integrate and later differentiate using a pencil stub on toilet paper. I recalled one of the Islamic sayings, that "Knowledge is an armour against enemies, an ornament amongst friends and your society in solitude." I strove to make knowledge my companion' (Isaacs 2010:129).

Isaacs came up with a term to describe the stay in solitary, 'eventless time'.

The timetable

According to Isaacs, there were two types of education on the island: political, and what he calls general or secular education. Political education was carried out by the organisations exclusively for their members. Isaacs was critical of this as it prevented the ability 'to learn from each other and to cross feed ideas' (Isaacs 2010:148). He was also critical of the content of the political education, which involved 'the rote learning of slogans and the simplified policy statements of the organisations. These utterances such as "one settler, one bullet" or "power to the people" or "to each according to his needs, from each according to his ability" were designed to rally, to maintain loyalty and boost the morale of the masses with not much thinking needed' (Isaacs 2010:150).

Instead, Isaacs turned his energies to general education:

> We had an illiteracy rate, I am sure – I had never measured it – but for me, I guess it was approximately 30 per cent of people there; mainly from the PAC, Poqo, who were not able to read, or read fluently. And, I thought that is now the first step. Get everybody literate and since I have an interest in mathematics, I got everybody to know it as well.

The education work quickly moved out of party political confines:

> We needed cooperation from everybody. Even Steve Tshwete was serving on that education committee with me and, later on, we went to serve on various other committees throughout our prison life there.

Within this formal education, which Isaacs developed with people like Tshwete and others, a teaching system emerged:

> I did not consider myself as too expert a teacher; I hardly taught for a year. But gradually people like Joel Gwabeni, Philip Silwana, Wellington Henge and Houghton Soci came, and who are expert teachers, and they took over much of the primary school classes, so that we could now concentrate on the secondary school.

In the teacher-student relationship, one would find that a younger person taught an older one and this led to complexities around seniority and tradition. But Isaacs says this was managed pretty well. The literacy classes were important. One of the motivations was to be able to communicate via letters with family:

> I think we motivated most of the students who were not able to read by saying: 'Look. The next letter you write home, you are going to try doing it yourself; even if you write the first, somebody else will add further to it. And when you received an answer, you are first going to try reading it yourself.' It was not as formally put. It was a type of

UNIVERSITY OF SOUTH AFRICA

This is to certify that

in the year 19 69

SEDICK ISAACS

obtained the Degree of

HONOURS BACHELOR OF SCIENCE

in the Department of

PSYCHOLOGY

* * * * * *

Vice-Chancellor

Among the degrees Sedick Isaacs obtained in prison was an Honours in Science. After his release, he completed his doctorate.

spontaneous idea which comes in a community situation which looks planned, but basically it is not really planned.

According to Isaacs, the teaching of history was difficult because of the lack of good books. This changed when Marcus Solomon got hold of *Old Africa Rediscovered* by Basil Davidson and it became compulsory reading.

There were organisational issues around timetables and exams. Putting a process and programme into place was helped by the presence of people such as Wellington Henge, Douglas Piti and Philip Silwana who were trained teachers.

> Basically, I think we all taught – whether it was music or art, or whether it was soccer. We became a teaching community – a mutual teaching community. But I think one of my major organisational achievements, which I like to think about and imagine it was useful, was the problem that we had very little study time. I came up with the idea that we work in the quarry and in the quarry the warders have very little control on who must do what work.

This led Isaacs to create a timetable

> with history class around the spades and the geography class on the stone-breaking side, and so on. We had a series of classes arranged like that. That way we got a little bit more time for reflective study because we had no papers, so you could think about what you studied the previous day. I said let us make it a bit more practical. The night before, you will go through the lesson for the following day as if you are going to be the teacher, so everybody will prepare as if he was going to teach. Then, when you arrive at your place of work, we will have a lottery – draw little straws – and the one with the shortest straw is the teacher. That worked so well that one can actually see it from the results that year when we first brought that thing in. From that time onwards, studying continued.

> Of course, if you were found with study papers then you were threatened with being charged for bringing a paper out – for using your study materials for unauthorised uses – so you had to be very careful with your papers. You couldn't bring in more papers, which meant you had to memorise your lessons much better. And since

you would be critiqued by other would-be teachers, you had better prepare very well. That worked so well with us that even in university, classes started like that. Wherever possible, I joined those who were doing Economics I or Political Science II, or other Unisa courses. It broadened my understanding and my knowledge a lot and I think it helped me even in my profession today where I am a methodologist and informatician. Well, in that way we became a learning society; a university.

While Isaacs is justly proud of their successes, he is also honest about the limitations, lamenting that so many prisoners did not go 'beyond a moderate level of reading and rudimentary writing' (Isaacs 2010:152).

It was not only prisoners who sought out Isaacs as a teacher. Prison officials also came knocking with sometimes hilarious results. In one case, Warder De Wet asked for help with his Domestic Science Matric studies. When it came to writing the exam, De Wet did not bother about the questions but simply wrote down everything Isaacs had told him. Isaacs's tormentor, Delport, also asked for help with Biblical Studies.

Throughout all this, Isaacs carried on studying, focusing on psychology alongside mathematics.

Psychology

Isaacs studied psychology for two reasons:

> I had conflict. I was going to study law. I was going to become a lawyer. I was going to do an LLB ultimately, and I wanted to do a BA through London University because it was still allowed at that time. Then I had a number of clashes with the prison authorities who were using law in a very negative way. I remember one day I was charged for something and the magistrate, who was a prison officer really, came along and he said to me, 'Oh, it is [you] again. You, I am going to fix you up inside there.' And when they got into the court room, I told the prosecutor the magistrate was accusing me; he was threatening me outside. He said, 'No, no, no. He is the magistrate when he sits here, but outside he was not the magistrate.' He was Major so and so. Then it struck me that law is actually a social construct and it can

be bent and turned around. I was more scientific-minded so I said, okay, let me give up law. Then I looked at criminals who were there. Many of the long-term prisoners had a vacant stare. I wondered whether we will end up the same way as these prisoners. I was very curious to see what the effect of long-term imprisonment was. The text book described it as 'listlessness, mental vacuity, neutralisation of effect, demotivated and almost like an empty mind' at the end of it all. I thought I am going to study. And, as we are a community, we need to study together. That all made me interested in psychology – psychology of education and psychology of normal behaviour – and I did a BA in psychology with mathematics added to it.

Maths and Physics

Mathematics is the archetype of beauty.

Johannes Kepler (1571–1630)

While studying mathematics, Isaacs was teaching it to others.

> ... it was Matric mathematics, and I managed to infuse mathematics to such an extent that the English teacher was complaining that we are just starting to think mathematics only. Various types of mathematic discussions like: 'A man sits on a train and the train goes at 100km per hour, and he fires a bullet out of a gun which also goes 100km per hour. Will the bullet and the train run at the same [speed]?' led to Vector Theory, and physics. I remember prison people discussing almost anything and that was a huge area of discussion. So, in that way, I think I infused my students with mathematics. When we came in from hard labour we were very dusty and one needed to have a quick wash down. Some of the students, who were there before, were so anxious to know more about geometry and algebra that they used to come – I think I was probably the only teacher who stood naked under the shower explaining some mathematics or even sitting on the toilet explaining to the other students some concept of geometry. It was a type of behaviour, which was so common, so intimate, that we shared almost all intimate moments, whether we liked it or not.

The bookkeeper

One of the funniest stories at the island had to do with the new library. As word went round that it was being established, it became clear that young warders thought it was madness ... The first evening after the work groups had arrived back, these warders came and peeped through our windows to confirm that the rumour was true. Some made revealing remarks like, '*God die Pokos sit op 'n stoel*' ('My god, the Poqos are sitting on a chair'). Indeed, this was actually the first time we had sat on a chair after nearly 18 to 24 months (one was allowed to sit on a bundle of blankets). (Mogoba 2004:43)

Isaacs was one of the first prisoners who helped organise and set up the library at Robben Island – the library that transformed learning at the prison.

I had completed an Honours degree and wanted to register for the Master's degree. I did the Honours degree (in Clinical Psychology) without the prison department knowing. I just smuggled my application paper out to Unisa, and they registered me. Then when I finished that, I thought I would do the same thing. I smuggled out my application paper for a Master of Science degree. But the university then wrote me a letter saying that they had been informed by the government that no postgraduate would be allowed in prison because 'we' haven't got facilities for that.

Isaacs registered for degrees in Information and Library Science and Mathematical Statistics with supplementary courses in Computer Science. When the International Red Cross visited the island, Isaacs indicated that he was studying Library Science, but the library was very rudimentary and he wanted to set it up properly:

But then I worked in the quarry, they said I didn't have a good prison record, and that it was not going to be easy to let me transfer to the library. Nevertheless, I was surprised that I eventually got this library job. Then, Moses Dlamini and I started reorganising the library. The first thing I did was set up a proper classification of books according to the Dewey system, because I was learning that, and setting up catalogues in terms of various subject headings. It was a real practical thing for me in this library science degree.

There were a couple of library books there – mostly novels – and I asked the commanding officer. I said the university sometimes got rid of old books and if we could be allowed to write to them. Again, that is when the International Red Cross was fresh in their minds, and they allowed it. I wrote a letter to the librarian at the University of Cape Town, who I had met before, and she remembered me and knew what type of books we wanted. She made a selection of books, put them in one or two boxes, and had them delivered to the docks. It finally arrived on Robben Island. But it had to be censored first, because they had to decide whether these books are suitable for prisoners or not. And it was very artfully packed and selected so as to take away the tension from books which might be more sensitive, or regarded as more political.

Sedick Isaacs in the library on Robben Island

The first book that came out was a book on anatomy. Lieutenant Naude looked at that book and actually swore at me and said, 'Are you sure that that is a bloody university you wrote to? How can they be so stupid?' He threw the book aside and said, 'Definitely not allowed.' I think he must have been a Calvinist type of religious person. The next book was *Capital* and he thought it was about money; it was actually *Das Kapital*, the English version of it. Because he presumed it was about money, it was approved. Of course, I had to watch these books very carefully because after they went on the shelves some people borrowed it and didn't want to return it. Now, interestingly, if the books were critical of communism, the communists would rather keep it away from [us]. So those types of problems also arose. And the other book that I still remember very clearly was a dictionary. Then this guy, Lt Naude, said, 'Bloody hell, a dictionary is not a reading book. You can't have it.' And he threw the dictionary aside amongst the other so-called 'banned' books.

The timekeeper

On Robben Island, Isaacs and other prisoners made certificates for the lower primary school students and would hand them out as the prisoners progressed with their education. They even had examinations.

Now that is another interesting thing. With examinations – June examinations or the final practice exam had to be done in a time limit, a two or three-hour exam. So I trained my students to work in time limits. I set the exams. First I counted the minutes off – one, two, three, four – but, Nelson Nkumane had a bright idea of making a water clock. He had an old tin with a little hole in it and something floating in it with a pointer. The can had a hole allowing the water to drip out and as the water level dropped, the pointer moved down against a time scale. And that is how we practised our exams. Having done that, we had exams and we congratulated people who passed. There were good marks and we had a type of a certificate issuing ceremony. By that time I was doing calligraphy; and I wrote all those certificates and got it signed by whoever taught the subject – and we issued these certificates. Later on we also issued people with pens as a type of reward. I had to engrave the pens. If the pens were normally

Parker pens or plastic Bic pens, I had a sharp needle and I scratched it out, then I filled it with whitening shoe polish. It became quite a number. People tell me that they still have their pens. It was also a type of memento of our stay on the island – these pens. I should have made a pen for myself, but I never did.

Isaacs remembers that there was great joy at graduation, especially when those at the lower primary or primary school would receive their certificates. The certificate was a strong motivator. According to Isaacs, Steve Tshwete said: 'Today we issue these certificates, but when we take over the government those others will become legal certificates because we are going to recognise it as a token of achievement.'

Isaacs subscribed to a number of journals including *National Geographic*, the *Journal of Abnormal Psychology*, *Scientific American* and *Archimedes*: 'We ran a Journal Club and this also proved an excellent method of mental stimulation' (Isaacs 2010:164).

Art and music

For Isaacs, being on Robben Island meant many positive outcomes:

It gave me a sense of achievement and a sense of living to the utmost. I tried to help make the community as normal as possible. The other projects which we had were art exhibitions. We were in an art competition and we would appoint the people who were going to be art critics. At the end we gave a prize to Natoo Babenia. He was so proud of it, he actually brought it out with him and he asked Nelson Mandela to finally authenticate it as a certificate which he won on the island. Later, I saw it. I was quite pleased that we were actually able to do things like that. We had music competitions, too. We had, I think, the most significant music competition, or not a competition, an achievement. We had an 80-person choir that practised the Hallelujah chorus. I bought three versions of it since my release. I listen to it – and I cannot detect the real grandeur; the real magnificence in these, the effect that was produced there on the island. People like Tshumi Ntutu and Bulisi Qengaleka were the choir masters and they took them through various phases of practice after school. Solomon Mabuse was the trumpeter and they finally produced that magnificent piece of music for a Christmas function – and I think it was so wonderful. Of course, I am prejudiced. When I listen to it I would say nothing beats it. I even still hear those sounds which they produced; just a bit of this Hallelujah chorus. Although I can't sing, I know the words.

Back on the mainland

I can frankly say that today I do not bear any grudges against anybody. We were after all in a war situation and I often wonder what we would have done if our roles (warders and us) were reversed. Would our better education, our consciousness of oppression and appreciation of human rights have made any difference? (Isaacs 2010:11)

Isaacs was released in September 1977. He got married to Maraldea. Isaacs had actually started correspondence with Maraldea in 1966. Two prisoners had gone for medical treatment to Somerset Hospital and were treated by Maraldea, a nurse. They cajoled Isaacs into writing a letter to her. Sixteen years later they married.

Banned, Isaacs made a living by selling eggs. In 1981 he secured a job at Groote Schuur Hospital and it provided the impetus for him to study for the MSc which was denied to him on Robben Island. He went on to complete a doctorate in medical biometrics and became head of medical informatics at the hospital in 1999. Informatics is the application of computing and statistical methods in medical research.

Talking to Isaacs in 2011 reveals his continuing commitment to teaching mathematics. He tutors Matric students on Wednesday evenings and on Saturday mornings.

He is involved with postgraduate students at the universities of Cape Town and the Western Cape. He is also president of the African Region for Informatics. Initially, the only member was South Africa, but under his leadership the membership has grown, with countries such as Nigeria, Ivory Coast and Mali joining.

I ask him the key to learning mathematics.

He points to his six-year-old granddaughter, Aanya. He started teaching her mathematics from the age of two. He counted steps with her. Then he started playing competitive games like walking on a plank. When somebody fell, they got an 'x', when they walked across they got a tick. Together they counted to see who won.

Teaching is about innovation, imagination, fun.

Conversation returns to the island. For Isaacs, education on the island was the key to his ideas about teaching and learning:

Thus, we lived and shared everything and in the process became educated in more than one sphere, which kept us sane in the inhospitable place called Robben Island. I think I got a wonderfully balanced education together with this sharing that we could not have obtained in any other place or time in our lives. (Isaacs 2010:165)

Against this backdrop, Isaacs wonders about the actions of 'the hard-nosed comrades' he shared so much with,

and who were so concerned with the welfare of the oppressed and who found their way into government, and have allowed South Africa to become the most economically disparate society in the world. I also cannot understand how they were conned into buying such extremely expensive white elephants, in the form of warships and warplanes, in the face of so much poverty, and rising infant mortality in our country reaching a level even higher than Afghanistan. (Isaacs 2010:202)

This kind of critique has not stopped Isaacs from spreading the word, from teaching mathematics to his grandchild and matriculants, and supporting doctoral students with their research.

Every day he carries the lessons of Robben Island in his fraying satchel.

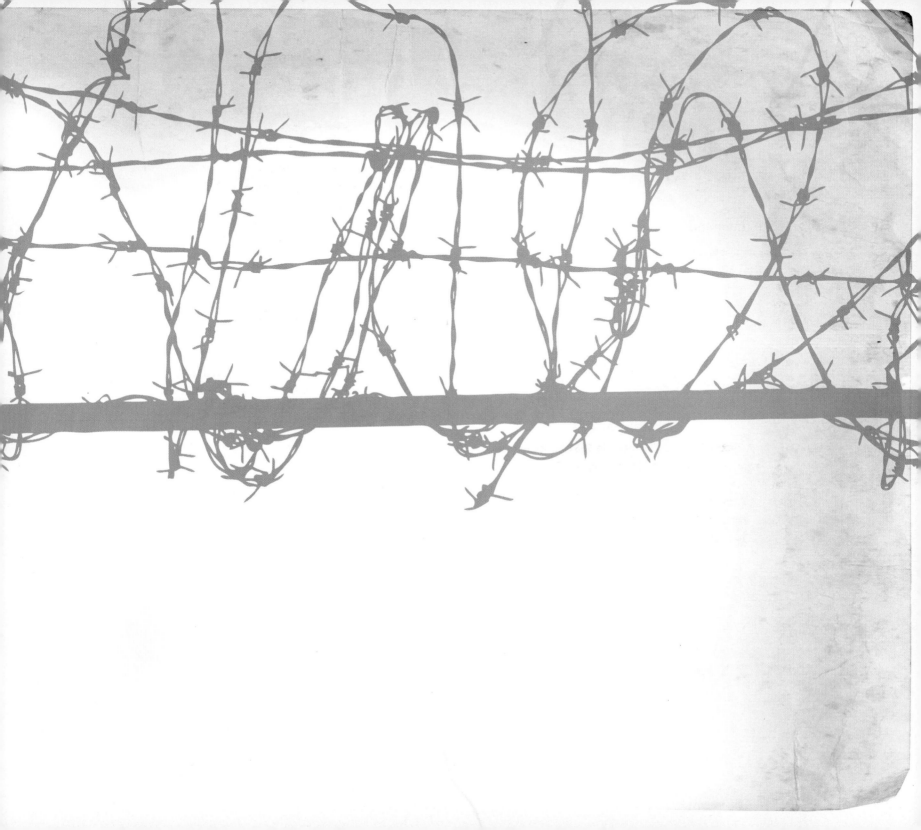

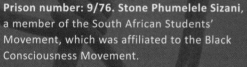

Prison number: 9/76. Stone Phumelele Sizani, a member of the South African Students' Movement, which was affiliated to the Black Consciousness Movement.

Stone Sizani's Masters degree in development studies.

University of East Anglia

School of Development Studies

At a Congregation held on 6 January 1995
the degree of Master of Arts in Development Studies
was conferred upon

Phumelele Stone Sizani

Derek C. Burke
Vice-Chancellor

Michael G E Paulson-Ellis
Registrar and Secretary

STONE PHUMELELE
SIZANI

The importance of mentors

Theory without practice is sterile and practice without theory is blind.

Stone Sizani

Without theory, action is blind; without action, theory is barren.

Vladimir Lenin (1870–1924)

Stone Phumelele Sizani[23] was among the stream of young people who were incarcerated on Robben Island in the aftermath of the uprisings of 1976. One of nine children, he was born in Alexandra where his father was a shop assistant. His father was insistent that they all receive an education:

> My father used to tell us when we were still young that he had no cattle, he did not have any property, he didn't have any money in the bank, and that, even if he wished, he couldn't leave us any inheritance, so all of us must strive to get the best education. He will strip naked if he had to support us through university.

While Sizani was a determined and conscientious student who sought to fulfil his father's ambitions of getting to university, he was soon caught up in the political turmoil of the mid 1970s. Sparked by student rebellions in Soweto, the Eastern Cape also erupted with schools being the central incubators of militant protest. Sizani was at the fore, travelling to schools across the Eastern Cape under the banner of the South African Student Movement (SASM), mobilising students and supporting the spread of boycotts. He was arrested on 7 January 1976, charged with terrorist activities and sentenced to five years on Robben Island. He arrived on Robben Island at the end of 1977.

A new generation was arriving on the island at this time. While many looked forward to seeing the old leaders of the liberation movement, there was a marked difference in the way this new influx of young activists sought to approach the island:

> Many young people – especially the group that came after 1976 – when they got onto Robben Island, they had that attitude of no 'education without liberation'. For them the line was that everything should be focused on liberation first and education would follow the defeat of apartheid. This was a different position to that taken by

the prisoners who had been there from the 1960s. They had fought against an attitude by the authorities that they should be left to rot and understand nothing. They struggled to be given permission to study and they had prevailed. When we got there they only had the right to study up to junior degree – not beyond. But, at least, they were able to study. They told us that they had fought for the right to study and that if young people think that education has no value in their lives they are mistaken. They took us through that history and the value of education in our lives. Young people said, 'We were burning schools in Soweto; we were burning schools where we come from. We can't betray those people now and come and study on Robben Island.' So the older folks were saying, 'No, you will study. It is good for you.'

Kathrada, one of those older prisoners, writes of this period in his *Memoirs*:

I spent a long time talking to the young prisoners who flooded into our midst and, more importantly, learning from them. It was painful to see so many bright and capable people being locked up for years when they should have been at school or university, carving out a future for themselves and for their people ... A number of the youngsters rejected study as a waste of time. Their priority was to achieve liberation, and everything else was of secondary importance. This was one area in which we should guide them, and we spent many hours persuading them that they should use their time in prison to equip themselves for the future. By and large we were successful and many of them did extremely well, and were grateful for the advice. (2008(a):277–278)

One of those youngsters was Stone Sizani. Studying was part of the broader approach to discipline. According to Sizani, there were two forms of discipline on the island, that of the authorities and that of fellow prisoners:

I learnt that there was a difference between the discipline taught by warders and the discipline taught by your own organisation. A big difference. Prison discipline would be to obey the regulations. But, if you obey the regulations in the face of prison warders, but break all the rules behind the scenes, you would still be okay because you would never be punished, nobody will arrest you, charge you or send you to the isolation section. Because nobody will know. But, if you obey the discipline of the organisation, it is the same as when Christians say: 'I will not commit sin because God can see me.' Even if you are alone, your conscience will tell you that you can't do this because God can see you. So they teach you that kind of discipline in the organisation. The kind of discipline that I am happy with is the discipline for self-thought – to read; to study. I don't know what I would have been, but the instinct through which we live our lives is unlike the kind of life you get trained for on Robben Island.

They taught you about everything. People went to get circumcised on Robben Island and understood what it meant. They got virtually everything about life. They understood. We got told and trained about everything – about the world in general; the economics of the world. During that time it was the Cold War period, so it was about which side the ANC was on. But then you were given an opportunity to go and read for yourself.

There is a second thing I like about Robben Island. It is that they train you not to rely on word-of-mouth alone. They train you to have a better understanding of the topic at hand by reading more about it. That is why the newspapers and radios on Robben Island – even though they were banned for a long time – were gold. People were prepared to pay quite a lot of money and bribe warders to bring in newspapers. It didn't matter how old a piece of newspaper was. Newspapers were such an important source of information to prisoners, such that some warders would wear political articles cut out of newspapers under their caps and bring it to a particular prisoner prepared to pay the price. That is how valuable information and education was on Robben Island.

'If you don't want to read you rust'

Some people on Robben Island could order books by virtue of the areas of study they were allowed. When the book arrived, either the whole book would be copied by hand – people would take shifts to write that book up. Of course, depending on how tired you were, you may miss a line; you may miss a page. But a book will be copied –

either a chapter or a whole book. People would sleep in shifts. You would write and then, when you were tired, another shift took over. That was how people valued books and education on Robben Island.

On arrival, there were other priorities. There was a thirst for what was happening on the outside. The news of the 1976 rebellion had given renewed hope to prisoners who had been incarcerated from the early 1960s and they were keen to hear first-hand of the uprisings across the country. But just as they shared news of the rebellion with prisoners who had been on the island from the early 1960s, so the older prisoners had an impact on their lives.

Sizani was convinced by older prisoners of the need to study. In a way he was fulfilling his father's wishes of getting an education, albeit under circumstances that his father did not envisage.

> I was encouraged to study, although I never went beyond Matric because I didn't have adequate monies to do so. But I wanted a chance to read more. By the time I got out of prison in 1981, I had studied philosophy, economics and history. I liked biographies best. I read many of them and I was able to have a better understanding of my life, my own self, and why our country was in a mess – which it was. I was encouraged to research more in order to assist other people. I was trained to go back into trade unions, into civil organisations and into political organisations. Hence, I participated in a leading role in the United Democratic Front (UDF) from 1983 until the time the UDF was stopped in 1989. Education in that context, is still valuable to me.

Alongside this, prisoners were siphoned off into their respective political organisations. In Sizani's case, his high school affiliations meant that he was first taken into the fold of the Black Consciousness Movement (BCM).

Once a prisoner's organisational affiliation was made clear, more senior members

> would then take you on a trip, maybe the whole year. Even though you may belong to the organisation that you claim to belong to, they would still take you on a trip around the rugby field to understand what you are saying about what you stand for and your activities. I was the chairperson of a branch of South Africa's student movement

[South African Students' Movement – SASM], which was an affiliate of the Black Consciousness Movement (BCM). So, the organisation that would receive you would be BCM. And then the BCM would take you along to examine your deeper understanding of black consciousness, philosophy and activities. Then, if they found that you needed fine tuning, you would be placed in a cohort. They would understand in which cohort you belonged, so they placed you there. There would be beginners who would have a huge class where lecturers would come and talk about that political party first. Then they would broaden the scope to cover the whole political spectrum of South Africa. Beyond that, they would give you books to read. The majority of the books that you were given to read were related to that political party and its own political influences. Then you would graduate depending on how fast you learned. Later you could freely mix with other political parties when your organisation sensed you have a better understanding of what you are doing.

Beyond the political lessons of history and the orientation of political parties, Sizani was also acquiring other lessons. One of them was about skills and expertise:

> You see, Robben Island taught me something: never ever try to be good at something you are not good at. You must specialise in the area of your efficiency; of your competence and do that to the best of your ability and leave the rest to other people who have a better understanding and better skills. But that is not the only thing we were taught on Robben Island. We did not learn only about politics. We learned about life in general.

Sizani differentiates three areas of life on Robben Island:

> When we were sentenced in September 1976 in Grahamstown High Court, we were sent to Leeuwkop for three weeks. After that we were sent to Robben Island. We got there in October and were released in the general section on 8 December. The older prisoners were saying, 'If you don't want to read, you rust.' What they kept hammering into us is that a politician who does not read is not good enough. He will deal with issues intuitively and not philosophically, and not theoretically. He will not be a skilled writer. And a politician who does not write – who does not prepare – is not good enough. *So*

they emphasised education. They looked at all the variances and they were saying again what we need to do – which is a second area; not academic training, but also *education about life*. If you can't interpret the environment in which people live; if you can't solve problems that people are facing because you lack the understanding of life in general, then you will not be a good leader. How do you expect to lead in a trade union, in an organisation or in a national liberation organisation, without understanding even intimate problems people are facing in the street where you live? Life in general will help you do that. Therefore, you must understand what life is. But they said there is a third area which is the actual broader *theory and philosophy of politics*. They emphasised that these three things will help you understand how and where we come from in our country, and where we must head. I don't know anybody who has been on Robben Island who does not understand that theory without practice is sterile and practice without theory is blind, because you must have a compass through which you navigate life. Therefore, philosophy in politics and philosophy of life, and the basics of education, are the most important things to guide all of us through life.

Sizani witnessed prisoners turning theory into practice:

There were those who could not afford to pay for their school fees. Even before you get your assistance from London – the money that was channelled through the families for our studies – other prisoners used to help. A prisoner, who used to help me a great deal on Robben Island, was Pata Madalane. He used to assist me to pay for education for my Matric subjects on Robben Island because I couldn't get the money fast enough for me to be able to write my Matric. Matric for me was the longest period because I would write two subjects, maybe one, depending on how much money is available – even though I may be good in some subjects, but I couldn't write them because I didn't have the money. They would help you through that battle, so that your academic training must help you with the philosophy of life; with philosophy of politics. Parallel to your technical training, there would be another form. Cohorts took you through the fields of your politics, and then there would be your academic training. Then there would also be a philosophy of life where somebody will take you around the rugby field and the person will talk about life in general. They would give you examples of leadership; give you history of other countries, and tell you why it is wrong morally for anybody to tell a lie; why it is wrong for anybody to do criminal activities. They used to share this experience in terms of their own experience on Robben Island and when they got there the Boers wanted them to be criminals. In fact, they put them in the same cells as criminals, deliberately trying to destroy them. It is only the discipline that assisted them and they would attribute that discipline to their leadership.

The mentors

Sizani points to four people who left a lasting impression on his political and intellectual outlook:

Dennis Skundla was one of the most disciplined individuals on Robben Island. He had little education. People feared and respected him for his insistence on discipline. So, it didn't matter whether he subjected you to a disciplinary code or not, people respected him. He understood everything that would bring the organisation into disrepute – unlike what we are experiencing now. And, because of that, he was placed in control of the cells. Then he was made a cleaner in the cells. Cleaners played a huge role – not only in discipline and not only in cleaning the cells, because hygienic conditions were important. Cleaners were the centre of the political organisation. Whoever circulated a document, they would be handed over to the cleaner of that political organisation, in that particular cell where they were to be used. You need discipline to be able to handle that material because it is banned material. It will be confiscated by the warders if found. If you talk too much, you have no secret in your chest. If you cannot control who you tell about the material, then you cannot be trusted. That is why they chose the most disciplined among members for the organisation. So Dennis Skundla would discipline us in terms of self control and self confidence. Even though you may wish to do certain things or want to say certain things, you would be trained not to. Many people, having understood that kind of discipline, became the best underground operatives.

For Sizani, it was not just discipline, but Skundla's pivotal role on the island that made him appreciate that people had different attributes and this would be harnessed in different ways inside an organisation:

> There will be a type of person who will be good on a public platform. There will be a type of person who will be good to operate an underground. There will be a type of person who would be prepared to control a petrol bomb or a hand grenade, or be able to shoot. There will be a different kind of person who will be a proper candidate for the organisation and go around the world and propagate isolation of South Africa. So they would train you to understand the differences between the characters of those individuals. He trained you to look at yourself and say, 'How do I fit into the scope of those things?' You don't purely become good at understanding yourself overnight. It is a process of learning and understanding yourself.

The second person Sizani identifies as a great teacher was Nkutsweyo Nzawo from the BCM. Nzawo brought an appreciation of culture and music:

> Everybody knew Nkutsweyo as Skaapkop. Skaap was gifted. He was gifted in cultural things, especially self-teaching and teaching others how to write; how to teach somebody who is completely illiterate how to read and write. He did not only teach that, he also taught how people can be taken to be trained to write or read music – all the musical notes, and play a key; understand all the keys and chords on a guitar. He was so good. He had the kind of patience that enabled you to understand yourself and what you are capable of doing. If you were interested in taking the flute or the guitar he would not say, 'No, no'. He would show you how it is done and then you would learn. And when you realise, *'This is not for me. I liked it because so and so is doing it. But, because it is not the kind of skill that I can develop, maybe I have the potential – but not to that extent.'* Then you go and look for something else.

But it was not just his skills as a teacher of music:

> Skaap had the kind of philosophy in life that enabled him to survive on Robben Island. He had a very violent temper. He was particular about a joke that was told by a warder and a joke told by a prisoner.

He never laughed when a joke was told by the warder, especially if it belittled black people. Even though other people would forget, he was always conscious of that. He was heftily built and he would hold warders' uniforms on their chests and show them out. But when it came to things like how he can help other people to achieve what is best in terms of their potential, he was a different animal. Understanding and very caring. He would also assist people with connecting with their families, especially those who were illiterate, up to a point where they were able to write to their families, themselves, and trace their families. I was privileged to have been close to him. The third person I think I should use as an example here is Sothomela Ndukwana.

Ndukwana, for Sizani, was somebody who did not rely on anyone else:

> Sotho was not highly educated. He was a worker. His wife was a domestic worker. But Sotho, whose mother was a nurse and father a school inspector, understood education and aspired to higher levels of education. Early on, when we got to Robben Island, he adopted an approach that he did not like the idea of being taught by somebody else. He preferred to read and train himself. It is good to live with that kind of person.

For Sizani, the most exemplary figure was Kgalema Motlanthe, who he still sees as an example. For him, Motlanthe was a philosopher par excellence because he used everyday language to discuss difficult and complex theoretical issues. He had a second quality:

> Patience. He had the kind of patience which would allow him to stay on one chapter maybe for three months, if the people in the class had not understood it. But he would also be very sharp in understanding who was lagging behind, and how a cohort will be selected. I am saying three things about Kgalema; firstly, the ability to translate theoretical information into ordinary language; secondly, the patience to take somebody along so that they can understand; thirdly, a good eye to identify potential among those who were learning with him. Even today, the majority of the teachers, if they were to be taken to a school where Kgalema Motlanthe taught, they would benefit most from his lectures on the philosophy of life. He was the best teacher. In my life, I select those four as my best teachers.

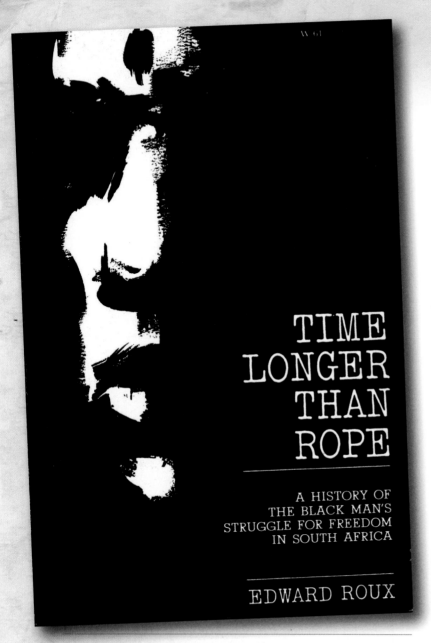

Eddie Roux's *Time Longer Than Rope*, a classic historical and liberation book, was for Sizani an important text for understanding South African history.

It was not just about teaching, it was also how people in the process were identified for particular tasks. In Sizani's case, he was earmarked to work in the kitchen and then as a 'postman'. The latter involved 'moving' material from one section of the prison to the other. This was important work and he was only given this task after he had shown the necessary qualities of discipline. For Sizani, this was the kind of thinking that lay behind deployment in contemporary South Africa by the ANC government:

> I am talking about how leaders in prison identified people. When everybody is talking about deployment and how wrong it is; how abusive it is; and how the other people abuse it, I worry about that because they know how it is done. They should know, because Kgalema was the best in that area.

While Sizani and other young people were studying and reading, they were also rebelling against the established and older BCM leadership, whom they felt sought to have a monopoly of the organisation. Sizani was one of those who felt that the BCM leadership with university training placed themselves above those who arrived with a high school education. This leadership felt that 'We must be kept at the high school level and depend on them to teach us what kind of information and philosophy we should learn. We rebelled against that.'

Sizani was also convinced that the BCM had arisen not to replace or challenge the ANC but to fill an important vacuum. When some members of the BCM saw themselves as separate to the ANC, he was one of those who chose to ally himself more closely with the ANC.

Post-prison

Robben Island stimulated Sizani's quest to study. After his release, he studied at the University of Port Elizabeth but soon fell foul of one of the lecturers.

> I couldn't last beyond June because I was able sometimes to contradict the lecturer. I remember we were doing some sociological subject and the lecturer said something historical, but also political. I

realised that he could have understood the topic better if he had read *Time Longer Than Rope* by Eddie Roux. Unfortunately, I told him so in the class and he felt undermined. Clearly I should have known better. I shouldn't have said that in the class and I shouldn't have told him in front of the students. But I did, and that was a mistake. From then onwards we didn't click well. Eventually I decided to quit.

The resurgence of politics in the early 1980s consumed Sizani's time. Sizani was a leading figure in the United Democratic Front (UDF) in the Eastern Cape, serving as regional treasurer. He was detained in 1986 and released in 1989.

Throughout this, the flame of studying fuelled by his father and the experiences of Robben Island never really died. He was eventually to obtain a Master's degree in Development Studies at the University of East Anglia in the United Kingdom.

After 1994, Sizani was to become a leading ANC figure in the Eastern Cape, serving as chairperson of the region and MEC for Education. He was subsequently deployed to the national parliament.

Sizani is open about the problems besetting education, having witnessed it first hand as an MEC (Member of the Executive Committee – a provincial minister) in the Eastern Cape. He identifies three problem areas:

> There is no schooling system because there is no school management, there is no school leadership, there is no discipline in the schools.

Sizani does not venture into a critique of the ANC government's approach to education, which has been marked by the adoption and summary rejection of policies such as outcomes-based education. His critique remains internal to the schools themselves. He is circumspect about advancing any substantive thoughts about the broader policy making environment and whether there is a lack of political will to change inherited patterns of inequality.

These are difficult times in the ANC with loyalty and 'revolutionary discipline' under constant scrutiny.

Post-apartheid and power

'What is different for you in terms of fighting a system and being in power now?'

> The difference lies in these two phrases: one, either you are an agent of change or a manager of change, that is where the difference is. When you are not in power and you are fighting the system so that it is fair and just and equitable to everybody, you are an agent of change, you must do something about it. And one of those things you will have to do to achieve that, is to mobilise, organise and make sure that people are agitated against the ills of society as an agent of change, and you do so without being an anarchist, you do so as a responsible organised person. The managers of change are those people who say, slow down, *wag 'n bietjie* (wait a bit), wait, wait, wait, for instance you are waiting for a house, it has been a housing list, you are told wait we are still doing that, even though money is there.

Managing change for Sizani is about understanding process and budgets and priorities, different from the apartheid days of mobilising and agitating.

Sizani continues to be an avid reader and spent a lot of time reading South African political biographies,

> but I have given up reading those books now. First they have given us the information and the background where we come from, but we need books now to take us forward, we need books that provide solutions to our current problems, not only South African problems, African problems and the world problems about development, why we have underdevelopment. So I am looking forward to reading books on the political economy of development.

Alongside this Sizani has started to read on the history of the Italian politics:

> In the process of my reading I came across books on the Mafia, the origin of the Mafia and how it operates now and these are the type of

books I am reading, so surprise, surprise, they give you insights how the economy of Italy is being run.

He worries too about the lack of intellectual engagement:

In South Africa these days, people don't speak to each other, they don't communicate, they shout at each other. If they disagree with you they will howl you into silence, they will marginalise you, because nobody wants to listen to your point of view, they want to listen to those that are agreeing with them. In democracies all over the world the first basic thing for an effective democracy is for us to allow other opinions to be viewed, because even if that opinion is bad, or even you disagree with it, it has to be measured against another one, so if it is suppressed how do you measure it. Intellectual discourse in South Africa is held back because there is no engagement, because very few people read these days, not in a manner in which you will read on Robben Island, you read and engage. For instance when you read a book, that is not enough, you must read and engage, read and engage, then your own intellectual capabilities are sharpened. Not only are you gathering more information, but the way you argue your points are sharpened all the time by engagement. Also there is no political education at all taking place now precisely because who is going to do it anyway. Who? Have you ever heard of political education, are you worried about political education, no, it is part of our business.

Prison number: 363/64. Neville Edward Alexander, a member of the National Liberation Front, signed off on two Sonnets (60 and 65) in Sonny Venkatrathnam's *Shakespeare*. (Portrait by Jurgen Schadeberg, 1994.)

NEVILLE EDWARD ALEXANDER

'Stop schooling, start educating'

Like as the waves make towards the pebbled shore,

So do our minutes hasten to their end

William Shakespeare, 'Sonnet 60'

In Venkatrathnam's *Shakespeare*, Neville Alexander[24] signed off on two Sonnets, 60 and 65.

O how shall summer's honey breath hold out

Against the wrackful siege of batt'ring days,

When rocks impregnable are not so stout,

Nor gates of steel so strong, but Time decays?

William Shakespeare, 'Sonnet 65'

Why the sonnets?

I had studied English 2 at the University of Cape Town and one of our most charismatic lecturers, Phillip Segal, had taught us Shakespeare, amongst other things. He made us understand *Hamlet* in a modern way, not as some sort of mediaeval story, and also helped us to understand the beauty of Shakespeare's sonnets. There were certain sonnets of Shakespeare's, like 'When to the sessions of sweet silent thought, I summon up remembrance of things past' and so on, which stayed with one. When you look at a sonnet like that, it is exactly what you're doing in prison, all the time. You are constantly reflecting on your life, on what's happened and of course you couldn't say it more beautifully in a sense, you couldn't describe that act of remembering more beautifully than Shakespeare. 'Since brass, nor stone, nor earth, nor boundless sea, but sad mortality o'ersways their power', again the power of the word, the power of writing. I think that's what Phillip Segal brought across to me and why those particular sonnets expressed so directly what we were trying to do in prison.

When it came to Shakespeare, Alexander had certain favourites:

More specifically *Henry V*, and partly because there are certain plays by Shakespeare which are very war-like and moving, very inspirational. 'Once more unto the breach', which I memorised and every now and again at Christmas time we would hold forth.

At Christmas, the prisoners put on the rudiments of plays, engaged in story-telling and sang:

> You'd get someone like Nelson [Mandela] getting up and telling a story in English in a very wooden way, and the moment he switched to Xhosa it was quite different. (Alexander, quoted in Schadeberg 1994:51)

Alexander remembers the plays of Shakespeare, Brecht and Sophocles. The latter got:

> people like Nelson immediately interested. You know, the struggle over the corpse and the importance of that in African tradition. I think those traditional dimensions of *Antigone* in particular, were something that attracted people like Nelson, you know, and also because they were written in a translated form, a very simple but profound English, and this had a direct impact on people's consciousness.

In his memoirs, Mandela recalls volunteering:

> to play Creon, an elderly king fighting a civil war over the throne of his beloved city-state. At the outset, Creon is sincere and patriotic, and there is wisdom in his early speeches when he suggests that experience is the foundation of leadership and that obligations to the people take precedence over loyalty to an individual … But Creon deals with his enemies mercilessly. He has decreed that the body of Polynices, Antigone's brother, who had rebelled against the city, does not deserve a proper burial. Antigone rebels, on the grounds that there is a higher law than that of the state. Creon will not listen to Antigone; neither does he listen to anyone but his own inner demons. His inflexibility and blindness ill become a leader. It was Antigone who symbolized our struggle; she was, in her own way, a freedom fighter, for she defied the law on the ground that it was unjust. (Mandela 1994:441–442)

According to Alexander, it was the act of theatre that also gave the prisoners a:

> sense of being together, the finding of one another and was probably even more important than the plays themselves. The fact that you had to memorise your part or you had to write it down and read it from the script. I think those activities were very significant. Most of us, including myself, had never done that before, so prison gave us that opportunity.

Christmas was a time which brought togetherness, a time to laugh:

> Walter Sisulu would ask Joe Gqabi, who had a wonderful voice: he would say to Joe, please sing *Fatima My Love*. Joe would start singing a very vulgar song, and then Walter would say, 'Agh, you know I don't mean that'. In other words, people looked forward to certain things particularly at that time of year.

The library

> [I]t is my opinion that a political prisoner must find ways and means of squeezing blood from a stone. The main thing is to do one's reading with a certain end in view, and take notes (if one is allowed to write).
>
> – Antonio Gramsci (quoted in Harlow 1992:20)

Neville Alexander was a voracious reader before arriving on the island.

He had a prodigious academic life, finishing a Master's at the University of Cape Town in 1957 at the age of 21, and four years later, a doctorate at Tübingen University in Germany. Alexander started teaching German at Livingstone High School in 1962. He came from a long line of teachers. His maternal grandmother was an Ethiopian slave rescued by a British anti-slave patrol. She was to eventually settle in the Eastern Cape and become a teacher at Lovedale and Cradock. His father was a carpenter while his mother also became a teacher, 'so there was a tradition in our family of teaching and so on, I took naturally to it'.

Alexander soon made his mark at the school with one student at the time commenting: 'At school you were encouraged to be free, and when I looked at Dr Alexander he was completely different to anybody I had ever seen. He was, he just looked so free'. (Quoted in Chisholm 1991:14)

But within two years at Livingstone High, Alexander was arrested, charged and sentenced to ten years on Robben Island.

In the first year of imprisonment, there was almost no access to books. In the second year, 1965, they were allowed access to the prison library indirectly. The prisoners were given a list from which they were able to select books:

> It must have been in 1965 that I started reading widely, deeply, mostly English literature, Dickens, Shakespeare. All those books, Thomas Hardy, George Eliot, you name it, all the classical novels.

Alexander was then able to expand his reading. He could read German and this allowed his selection of books to increase tenfold. His colleague at Livingstone High School, Gustav Ascher, who taught German with him,

> made a donation specifically to the Robben Island library of books written in German in the full knowledge that eventually I would have access to these books. You see, it was just a treasury, Schiller and all the classical German stuff, but history, particularly the history of the Russian Revolution, Ricarda Huch's seminal study of the 1848 revolutions, stuff that even outside, you know, I would have had difficulty finding. So, from about '65 onwards, we had access to that type of material.

> I read Shakespeare from cover to cover, I had the complete works of Shakespeare and I left that on the island. We certainly left a whole lot of books there. In fact there was a quarrel about why I should take Trotsky's [History of the] Russian Revolution out with me, the reason being that I wrote a whole lot of stuff secretly into the book, which I needed to take with me. We had a whole argument about it, you know, that's the one book that is going out with me.

Debating Mandela

Government spokesperson Jimmy Manyi created a storm in 2011 when he suggested that there was an 'oversupply' of Coloureds in the Western Cape, and said a similar thing about Indians in KwaZulu-Natal. Neville Alexander entered this debate with a devastating counterattack, titled 'Race is skin deep, humanity is not'. (Cape Times, 5 April 2011)

In the article, Alexander points out that words such as 'oversupply' signal how:

> The dehumanisation of language and discourse corresponds to the dehumanisation of stigmatised persons. Once the commodity value of people displaces their intrinsic human worth or dignity, we are well on the way to a state of barbarism.

For Alexander, Manyi's outburst presented a challenge to:

> bring back into our paradigms, and thus into our social analyses, the entire human being and the ways in which human beings can live fulfilled lives beyond their mere economic needs, we will continue to promote anti-human philosophies and policies that ultimately tend to work to the benefit of those who have, and to the detriment of those who do not have.

At the outset this meant:

> You cannot fight racial inequality, racial prejudice and race thinking by using racial categories as a 'site of redress'. It is a fundamental theoretical and strategic error to try to do so by perpetuating racial identities in the nonsensical belief that this will not have any negative or destructive social consequences.

Alexander was in a sense returning to a prolonged debate about 'race' on Robben Island some three decades before. It began when his political grouping, the National Liberation Front (NLF), asked Walter Sisulu:

> to present a history of the ANC, since having come from the Unity Movement background, we knew very little about the real history of the ANC, we had a very prejudiced view and he gave us a serious lecture at the quarry.

This series of lectures led to questions on 'race':

> When we came to the Freedom Charter, the Kliptown Congress, Les van der Heyden asked Walter, but you know Walter, point number two of the Freedom Charter, all national groups should have equal

rights, we don't believe in that, what does it mean, can you explain what it means, the national groups, you are talking about. Walter said it's Africans, Coloureds, Indians and so on and Les said, no, no but look, we don't believe in this stuff you know, we need some proper explanation on this. So Walter, who was the epitome of modesty, said I can't really explain this to you, I am not a theoretician, why don't you ask Nelson to do that. And this is a very interesting story, because when we approached Nelson and said that Walter referred us to him, would he be prepared to give us a few lectures on the issue of the national question, I don't think he called it that, but on point number two of the Freedom Charter. He then said, well Neville, while I am prepared to have a discussion with you, I'm not prepared to have a public discussion. I said listen why not; the guys are really genuinely interested. He said well, you know the Freedom Charter is a sacred document (they may not be his exact words) and if any Congress member would think there was something shaky about that, it wouldn't be good for our movement. And this is typical Nelson Mandela by the way, typical of his approach, 'it wouldn't be good for our movement so I prefer to have a one-on-one discussion'.

Alexander reported this back to his comrades. Most were not happy, but Fikile Bam said:

Look, it's better for us to know than not to know. Let Neville have this dialogue. As a result we had this two-year long discussion, one day a week and lots of reading in between.

This legendary dialogue started with a simple but firm question from Mandela:

He asked me what our problems were around point two of the Freedom Charter. I said that from our point of view, the notion of four national groups or proto-nations is simply not acceptable, quite apart from the fact that on a purely conceptual basis, it would be very difficult to justify. Initially you had Khoi, you had slaves et cetera, and later on you had Coloureds. That was a sociohistorical construct and I said that this is the reason why the Unity Movement has the slogan, 'Let Us Build a Nation'. It was counter to the Afrikaner nationalist idea of an ethnic nation. The idea is to build as a political entity, a political

community, a South African nation, but this has to be built out of what was there before.

The discussion first took place in the quarry and then later in the rooms set aside for table tennis:

We presented what we thought to one another, or responded to questions, so there was a Socratic dialogue which took place over a few hours, at most two to three hours a day, per week.

Mandela's response to Alexander was to enquire whether:

the African people, meaning the Bantu-speaking, pass-bearing people of South Africa, he didn't use this term of course, the African people are not a nation. I said yes, I don't think one can speak of them as a nation, the fact that people shared a particular level and degree of oppression doesn't necessarily turn them into a nation, they might have common desires to get rid of the past but that doesn't turn them into a nation.

Things got heated and the dialogue nearly ended:

He said to me, if that's your view, I think there is no point in us discussing it any further and so you know, it was *stamp en stoot* (full of posturing) at the beginning. I had a similar reaction when he argued that a coloured person is the progeny of white and black, but that's nonsense, historically that is nonsense and conceptually not acceptable, and so on and so on. I also said then you know that we can't continue discussing if that's how you see this, you need to see it in a dynamic way, that's when I explained that for example, you started with slaves and Khoi et cetera, and the majority of so-called coloured people are derived from that particular lineage rather than from a mixture of white and black. We learnt though to be quite tolerant, accept certain things and put them into brackets, come back to them later. Anyhow, what happened was very interesting because as we went along, obviously we got more and more into the theory of nationality, theory of ethnicity and it meant reading and returning to the debate. By that time I had access to quite a few books as did Nelson, because I was studying Honours in History and the authorities were very interesting in that they allowed us all prescribed and some recommended books, so we would really manipulate and twist things.

106

I mean you would find a reference to Trotsky's *History of the Russian Revolution* in one or other book and say it's a recommended book and they would let you have it. As a result of that, we were then able to read and also discuss national struggles in other parts of the world. So it didn't simply revolve around South Africa. However, we looked at Afrikaner nationalism and specifically of course at the ANC and All African Convention and Unity Movement, and how their conceptions of nationality developed and so on. Eventually we agreed to disagree, I think would be the right thing to say.

Teaching and learning

Alexander's discussions with Mandela made him realise his lack of knowledge of African history:

What we knew about African history, was really the history of Europeans in Africa. And as a result, he influenced me to begin a serious study of African history. On the other hand, I'm not sure that Nelson would even admit that he was influenced by that discussion in any particular direction. But for them eventually to adopt the discourse of non-racialism as they did, whether they put it down to the UDF or not, it's quite interesting because certainly at that stage, he was very clear on a multiracial set-up, as were people like Walter Sisulu and others. The one-to-one discussion that led to many other discussions, it was not as systematic but raised the issues of armed struggle, participation in government created bodies.

Alexander also learnt from Mandela:

The Sisulus, Mbekis, all of the older men were really people of great dignity, great presence. You may have had very serious political differences with them in your own mind; nonetheless you came to respect their consistency, their breadth of vision, their minds, and their willingness to see you as somebody who actually had something to teach, although you were very much younger. I think those sorts of things stay with one, and certainly affected me for the better, for the rest of my life. (Lodge & Nasson 1991:310)

At the outset the classes were done:

on a one-to-one basis because at that early stage we were still under very sharp scrutiny by the authorities. Because people like myself and Les didn't know Xhosa well enough, we always worked in twos or threes, so there would be somebody who knew Xhosa and English who could assist us. We three would then stand working together and basically I would teach how to read, and because we weren't allowed to have paper, we used to write in the sand in the lime quarry. All the sort of instinctive, intuitive stuff of how you teach somebody to read and write, because I was a teacher, I had some background knowledge. We used various methods without realising at the time what we were doing, until we were allowed writing material in 1966.

Sometimes, the teaching of history had its limits:

I taught Clarence Makwetu, the PAC leader, and I will never forget when we discussed, for Matric purposes, the Suez Canal. I said to him, Zikali, we called him Zikali, do you realise that before the Suez Canal there was no such thing as Africa as a geographical entity, you know that it was part of the Eurasian, European land mass. He said, what do you mean? I will never forget this. He said, are you suggesting that there was never such a thing as Africa before 1869, so I said, ja, you know it's just a geographical expression. He said, Doc, he called me Doc, can I make a suggestion. I said of course, what's the suggestion? His response: let us never discuss this again.

How did lecturers at the University of South Africa deal with students like Alexander who already had doctorates and a profound knowledge of the subjects they were studying? It led, as in the case of Alexander, to surprising results.

Alexander remembers a history essay he wrote on the authentication of documents. He chose the Dingane-Retief Manifesto. This document purportedly showed that Dingane handed over land to Retief:

I applied all the criteria for authenticating the document. Then I found that out of the five or six criteria that you have to have, this document didn't satisfy one of those criteria, not one. So I wrote back and said how is it possible that in our history books this document is taken as a point of departure for explaining how the land came into the hands of the Boers. When clearly from the point of view of authentication, this is not an authentic document. The professor didn't respond directly, he gave me something like 95–97% for my essay. All he said was: you have raised a number of very important questions.

Many years after his release from the island, Alexander met one of his former lecturers, Professor Floors van Jaarsveld. Van Jaarsveld had made national headlines when he had been tarred and feathered by the white right wing for questioning the Afrikaner nationalist story that God had interceded on the side of the Voortrekkers in the 1838 battle against the Zulus. Van Jaarsveld told Alexander what they had learnt from essays such as his:

> We were trying to tell you guys how to write history but the essays produced from Robben Island opened our eyes to so many things. Some of us realised that what they were trying to do wasn't just wrong, but actually immoral in scholarly terms.

After the island, Alexander came to be involved in organisations with an avowedly socialist outlook. He was part of an activist intellectual tradition that characterised South Africa as an example of racial capitalism. Alexander was one of the driving forces of the Cape Action League (CAL) that joined with black consciousness organisations to form the National Forum (NF) in 1983. Its Azanian Manifesto declared itself for 'a democratic, anti-racist and socialist Azania' (Lodge & Nasson 1991). While the NF was supposedly in opposition to the SACP's Soviet Marxism, in reading through the documents and speeches of the NF one gets a sense that it was also trespassed by what John Saul, writing about countries such as Mozambique, labelled a 'pre-packaged Marxist-Leninist pedagogy' that was 'frozen … mechanical and lifeless' (Saul, quoted in Nash 1999: 78). The NF failed to attract into its ranks any substantial sections of the organised working class and was overshadowed by the United Democratic Front which sought to identify with the Freedom Charter and the Congress tradition.

In the 1990s Alexander was a leading figure in the Workers' Organisation for Socialist Action (Wosa). This organisation also failed to capture any mass support as the unbanned ANC gobbled up the mass democratic movement and the support of Cosatu (Congress of South African Trade Unions).

What of Alexander's vision of a South Africa 'where the interests of the workers shall be paramount through worker control of the means of production, distribution and exchange'? This vision seems as remote more than two decades after the unbanning of the liberation movements as it did when Alexander was incarcerated on Robben Island.

But still Alexander fights on for a new, more equitable South Africa on a terrain he knows well.

Educating the present

Alexander, who has spent a considerable amount of his post-Robben Island life involved in basic adult education, is scathing about where the country is in the present conjuncture when it comes to education:

> I think one has to be brutally honest. First of all, I think that the opportunity given to us in 1993–94 was completely wasted. When the issue of outcome-based education came up, some of us said right at the beginning, let's take this easy, take it slowly because teachers are not prepared for this kind of syllabus. From what we understand, it failed elsewhere, so why are we doing this. There were alternative ideas out there, but I think there was an insistence especially from the trade union lobby of integrating education and training. I think people were misled by a very modern, very sophisticated concept which at that stage we were not in a position to implement, with the result that the schools with resources could simply go ahead and those that didn't have [resources], stagnated. To be quite frank with you, I think the system of education is in a complete mess, and no matter who the Minister of Education is at the moment, unless they change the system, they cannot improve much and I mean in the Western Cape they are spending a lot of money on technology, on computer labs and so on, they are not educating the kids, they are schooling them. The kids are not going to come out as critical learners, critically aware, politically and otherwise, they will know

Es 3

Naam/Name	ALEXANDER: N.E. (Mr)	Kursus/Course	History
Datum Ingeskr./Date of Entr.	18th Feb. 66	Ras/Race	Coloured
Graad of Diploma/Degree or Diploma	Honours B.A.	Verw. nr./Ref. No.	A.879

Taak Assignment	Datum Date	Punte Marks	Kommentaar Comment

SECTION C   SUBJECT ENROLMENT FOR THE CURRENT YEAR 19___
(Block Letters)

NAME (Mr./Mrs./Miss) Neville Edward Alexander   Ref. No. A 879.

ADDRESS ROBBEN ISLAND PRISON, ROBBEN ISLAND.   Race Col.

Course Hons. B.A.   Date of Birth 22nd October, 1936   Occupation Imprisoned-Teacher

Subjects	Language medium E. or A.	(For office use only)
1. Theoretical History: Outlines of historical method and theory, and historiography from the 18th cent.	E.	
2. The Cape under Van Riebeeck and the Van der Stels	E.	
3. The American Revolution and the formation of the Federal Constitution 1763-89	E.	
4. Nationalism and Internationalism in the 19th and 20th centuries.	E.	
5.		
6.		

Neville Alexander, who already had a doctorate before his incarceration, also studied for a History Honours degree at Unisa in the late 1960s. His marks, mostly distinctions for his essays, and his correspondence with lecturers Floors van Jaarsveld and Ben Liebenberg are on file in the History Department at Unisa.

of History.

22nd February 1966.

Mr N.E. Alexander,
Robben Island Prison,
Robben Island.

Dear Mr Alexander,

Welcome to our honours course. I hope that you will derive both pleasure and profit from you studies.

I am sending you the tutorial matter for paper 1 (theory of history) under separate cover. Included in this tutorial matter you will find a number of tutorial letters from previous years which may be of assistance to you.

You may start working on paper 1 immediately and as soon as you have completed it (or nearly completed it) we shall supply you with the material for the next paper. Please let us know when you are ready.

In tutorial letter no. 2 of 1963 (still valid) you will find a list of the assignments you should send in for paper 1. You will note that there are seven assignments and we expect you to send in one every three weeks. The closing date for your first assignment will therefore be three weeks after the receipt of this letter and for the rest of the assignments every three weeks thereafter - you may, of course, let us have the assignments sooner.

Professor F.A. van Jaarsveld is responsible for the first paper and should you encounter problems in the course of your studies in this paper you should not hesitate to contact either him or me. You may be sure we shall do all we can to assist you.

Yours sincerely,

B.J. LIEBENBERG.

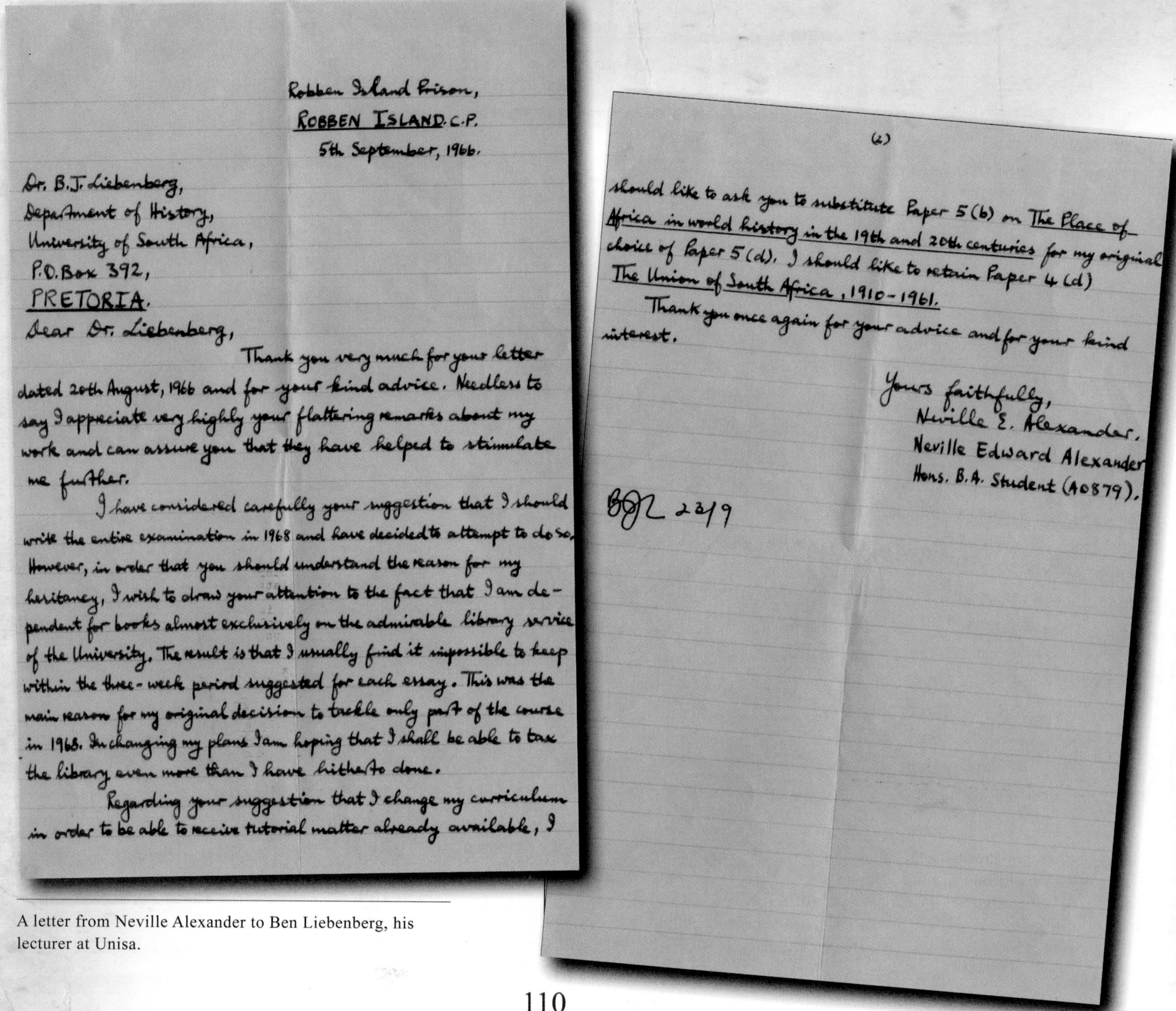

Robben Island Prison,
ROBBEN ISLAND. C.P.
5th September, 1966.

Dr. B. J. Liebenberg,
Department of History,
University of South Africa,
P.O. Box 392,
PRETORIA.

Dear Dr. Liebenberg,

Thank you very much for your letter dated 20th August, 1966 and for your kind advice. Needless to say I appreciate very highly your flattering remarks about my work and can assure you that they have helped to stimulate me further.

I have considered carefully your suggestion that I should write the entire examination in 1968 and have decided to attempt to do so. However, in order that you should understand the reason for my hesitancy, I wish to draw your attention to the fact that I am dependent for books almost exclusively on the admirable library service of the University. The result is that I usually find it impossible to keep within the three-week period suggested for each essay. This was the main reason for my original decision to tackle only part of the course in 1968. In changing my plans I am hoping that I shall be able to tax the library even more than I have hitherto done.

Regarding your suggestion that I change my curriculum in order to be able to receive tutorial matter already available, I

(2)

should like to ask you to substitute Paper 5 (b) on The Place of Africa in world history in the 19th and 20th centuries for my original choice of Paper 5 (d). I should like to retain Paper 4 (d) The Union of South Africa, 1910-1961.

Thank you once again for your advice and for your kind interest.

Yours faithfully,
Neville E. Alexander,
Neville Edward Alexander
Hons. B.A. Student (A0879).

BQR 2319

A letter from Neville Alexander to Ben Liebenberg, his lecturer at Unisa.

110

how to set up a business plan or whatever and to hell with it, that's not what education is about.

For Alexander, the time has come to:

review some of our cherished notions, what's coming in our report that the Centre [Project for the Study of Alternative Education in South Africa at the University of Cape Town of which Alexander is the Director] has suggested the need to change the way teachers are trained, instead of this sort of theory-based system, where you come to a lecture and you learn a whole lot of theory, then you are expected to go and apply it in the classrooms, to base it on a mentorship, apprenticeship system the way you train artisans you know, that's the way you train teachers. There are a whole lot of other issues. I've written these articles, one is called, 'How to Organise a Soft Landing for South African Education', and I think what I'm getting at is that we probably, especially now with the Zuma administration, I hate the word, but I'll use it, have a window of opportunity for reconsidering where we're going.

Reading clubs

I am somewhat less interested in the weight and convolutions of Einstein's brain than the near certainty that people of equal talent have died in the cotton fields and workshops.

Stephen Jay Gould (1941–2002)

Saturday mornings often see Alexander in Langa, participating in reading groups. The reading groups were stimulated when a community organisation in Langa sought the support of the Project for the Study of Alternative Education in South Africa in addressing children's literacy. After much discussion:

Neville Alexander's grades for his History Honours essays, submitted to Unisa in the late 1960s.

we suggested a reading club … we started the whole thing at the end of 2006, beginning of 2007. After a few months I realised what we are trying to do in a working class community is to recreate conditions that would stimulate the love of reading and writing amongst young children from age 3–4 up to age 14–15, you know, stimulate the love of reading which would normally occur organically in the middle class home. The middle class home where people are literate, they have internet, there's a lot of books et cetera and children just take naturally to reading and writing, unless there are extraneous things like unsupervised television. This is what we are trying to do. It doesn't exist in most working class homes even though there is a veneration for education, the conditions simply are not conducive to children organically acquiring the love of reading and writing, and what we are trying to do now is to take the most advanced, the most enlightened elements of the community and put them together once or twice a week with children and create that environment. That's the basic principle of these reading groups.

Everything is bilingual. We have new clubs in different parts of the province where it's trilingual, where kids are speaking English, Afrikaans and Xhosa. Otherwise it's Xhosa-English or Afrikaans-English. We get books, age appropriate books and in a stress-free playful environment, we get kids to want to read, we get them to listen to stories, to tell stories, to write them down, so they see the link between speech and writing et cetera., and generally speaking, we take some of the most well-known stories, translate them into Xhosa and or Afrikaans and publish them. If we are not allowed to publish, we photocopy them, kids read them and children begin to write their own things, so we publish their little books. The result is that in a place like Langa, we now have an average of 170–200 children, every single Saturday morning, and we've organised it very well. We have up to 30 volunteers every week, high school children, students whom we recruit, as well as parents who come to help. We do get a few teachers, mostly young parents and high school students, and then of course university students come and help with the reading and writing. So on average we have a 1 to 4, 1 to 5 relationship at these groups on a Saturday morning. Currently, there are about 25 such

reading clubs or reading groups in the Western Cape and elsewhere in South Africa, and they are growing by the day.

Island legacy

[W]e were very well prepared by Robben Island, and I would say for myself that not a single year was wasted. (Alexander, quoted in Lodge & Nasson 1991:311)

Alexander is still a voracious reader:

I've been reading Eric Hobsbawm's book called *Changing the World: Marx and Marxism 1840–2009*. It goes back to the Feuerbach thesis [that] it's not enough to interpret the world we have to change it. Hobsbawm deals with the legacy of Marxist thought and activism. It's not terribly well written unfortunately. Then a book I've just started reading, a really fascinating book by John Holloway, *Changing the World without Taking Power*. He is an anarchist but I think he really puts things in perspective, and then as far as novels are concerned, I've been reading Robert Harris on *Cicero* and a whole series of things on the Roman republic, very fascinating. On a lighter note, I've been reading Margie Orford's detective novels which are situated in Cape Town.

For Alexander, one of the seminal experiences of the island was 'the struggle to know yourself' (Schadeberg 1994:51). This process was liberating at a very personal level:

You got to love other men in ways that previously you'd never have thought possible. It wasn't just ordinary friendship, but a need for another's company, a need to communicate, even to feel one another sometimes. I remember the warmth that somebody putting his hand on you could communicate, the sense of support and solidarity that was in the gesture. I think of those things and the naturalness of it. Outside, one was always straitjacketed by convention. Men didn't do those things, and it was a liberation, a process of liberating yourself from a convention, an outmoded, reactionary convention. (Alexander, quoted in Lodge & Nasson 1991:309)

THE SIXTH ACT?

If one has once read Shakespeare with attention, it is not easy to go a day without quoting him, because there are not many subjects of major importance that he does not discuss or at least mention somewhere or the other, in his unsystematic but illuminating way. Even the irrelevancies that litter every one of his plays – the puns and riddles, the list of names, the scraps of 'reportage' like the conversation of the carriers in *Henry IV*, the bawdy jokes, the rescued fragments of forgotten ballads – are merely products of excessive vitality. Shakespeare was not a philosopher or a scientist, but he did have curiosity, he loved the surface of the earth and the process of life – which it should be repeated, is *not* the same thing as wanting to have a good time and stay alive as long as possible. (Orwell 1969:116–17)

Three and even four decades after they read Shakespeare on Robben Island, prisoners can still remember the plays and sonnets that moved them, and quote lines from them. They read these works in ways that made sense to their own life experiences and the sociopolitical circumstances of the time. When peasants from the Transkei, jailed for fighting against the confiscation of their land, listened to JB Vusani recite lines from King Lear, they could relate as much as they struggled to understand why

Lear did not consult with his elders. Kwedi Mkalipi rationalised his own refusal to accept early release if it meant compromising with apartheid by seeking strength from the words of Lady Macbeth:

> All the perfumes of Arabia will not sweeten this little hand.
>
> *Macbeth*, Act V, Scene 1

It was not only the political reading of Shakespeare that inspired, but also the beauty of words, as Neville Alexander reflects when he recites lines from Shakespeare's Sonnets some three and half decades after he signed Sonny Venkatrathnam's *Shakespeare*.

Books were 'chewed', reflected upon, debated, and absorbed with a passion. The sections chosen by prisoners in Venkatrathnam's Shakespeare speak at once to different emphases, to different generations even, but importantly to how people from different political traditions, who debated vigorously and often displayed a deep sectarianism, could come together around an appreciation of a common text. As Saths Cooper puts it, 'there is something for 'Everyman' (in Shakespeare), whether in tears, laughter or other tribulations and joys'.

Books opened new ways of seeing while allowing prisoners to escape the prison walls. Given the limited number of books available, many prisoners read the same books over and over again, often deriving new meanings, reminding us that while 'we can read a book again, starting over as Plato believed souls might start over again in life ... it is also true, as Heraclitus might have said, that the same person never reads the same book twice' (Scholes 1989:19).

As prisoners taught others the art of reading and writing, this 'education' opened a whole new world. For the first time many prisoners read and wrote their own letters, a vital means to 'escape' to 'home'; 'as your letter opens/there is an unfolding of sky, or word from the outside/of memory' (Breytenbach 1984:305).

Listening to the stories of Robben Island prisoners, one gets a profound sense of the way that they visualised freedom. It was not just a matter of defeating apartheid and gaining the vote, but also one of addressing poverty and inequality; *So that distribution should undo excess/And each man have enough.* These were not just technical issues but the grand narratives of national liberation, practising non-racialism, and the empowerment of people. This is why every prisoner emphasised the literacy classes that opened the world to their fellow inmates. The re-imagining of the prison was also a re-imagining of a new society.

The value of speaking to Robben islanders is that it involved listening to people who lived in two temporal zones. Behind bars, on the rough end of power, but driven by the ideal of a new South Africa. And then, abruptly, into the zone of an apartheid-free country. 'When biographically lived time crosses collective time – this historical conjuncture marks a generation ... born twice' (Buck-Morss 2010:76).

Thomson Gazo, inspired by a messianic spirit, set out from Cape Town to assassinate the Bantustan leader, Kaiser Mantanzima. While that mission ended in failure, he feels that with the fall of apartheid, his objectives have been accomplished and he spends a great deal of his time on church matters. This 'retreat' to the power of the Almighty probably has a lot to do with *the fall* of his organisation, the PAC. Monde Mkunqwana dreams of flying and appreciates that in the new South Africa his grandchildren can make those dreams become a reality. Sedick Isaacs still teaches mathematics with the same passion that he exhibited almost fifty years ago on Robben Island. His grandchild is his latest student.

Stone Sizani survived the internecine warfare that haunted and continues to haunt the ANC in the Eastern Cape. Once the provincial minister for education in the Eastern Cape, he was redeployed to national parliament. Sizani, whose biography through the apartheid years speaks to the commitment to organise people as agents of change, now sees the importance of managing expectations, and putting in place systems and procedures of governance; people need to exercise patience. Sonny Venkatrathnam lives Lear at the end of a cul-de-sac in Durban, tending his roses. He keeps his *Shakespeare* close by, a remembrance of what was and what will never be in his lifetime.

Prisoners occupied tiny cells cut off from the outside world, 'a complete world, a life complete in itself, without a reference to anything outside itself' (Lewin 1976:50). Orwell has written that 'the imagination, like certain animals, will not breed in captivity' (1969:174). But *contra* Orwell, through books prisoners escaped, their imaginations letting them travel the world. 'All the world's a stage', it seemed, as prisoners devoured the lessons of the Bolshevik, Vietnamese, Cuban and Algerian struggles.

Their own biographies are a testimony to the zeal, idealism and courage to bend history under the most constraining of circumstances.

Many had a sense that they were living through their own revolution when Nelson Mandela was inaugurated as President of South Africa on 10th May 1994. It was an epochal moment of the late twentieth century, capturing the imagination of freedom-loving peoples all over the world.

There was much anticipation among the masses that the leaders of the new social order would devote themselves to redressing the evils of apartheid and the reconstruction and development of a New South Africa.

The political landscape began to change with bewildering speed. The Mass Democratic Movement (MDM), which had spread across the country through the 1980s, displaying remarkable levels of local innovation and power, was absorbed into the ANC. This liberation movement would now filter the ideas and demands for change upwards into a new government. Liberation fighters were integrated alongside apartheid apparatchiks working the levers of institutional power. Natural attrition would gradually see the sun set on the latter. The state would lead this process of 'transformation' and 'redress', to use the parlance of the time.

But the headiness of the four years after Mandela's release were tempered as the ANC readied for power. As the ANC's Pallo Jordan points out:

> Virtually all the liberation movements that attained victory after 1947 (the attainment of Indian independence), including our own, have been forced to make compromises at the point of victory. National liberation has rarely come in the form that the movement sought. Consequently, the terrain on which the triumphant movement has to manoeuvre after victory is not necessarily all of its own choosing or making. (Quoted in Magubane 2004:658)

The ANC came to power when the global terrain had changed dramatically. Most significantly, the Soviet Union had collapsed and historians were heralding the 'end of history', with capitalism as the only viable alternative (Fukuyama 1992). This was the position taken by those wielding power in post-apartheid South Africa. Mandela who, in his first speech after his release from prison, had defended nationalisation, returned from Davos in Switzerland in 1992 to announce to his closest aides: 'Chaps, we have to choose. We either keep nationalisation and get no investment, or we modify our own attitude and get investment' (Sampson 1999:435). It was symptomatic of a time where 'even some of the most fervid foes of the apartheid regime formally conceded to the "natural" (if not supernatural) power of global markets and to the claim that, because of globalization, "there is no alternative" (TINA) to orthodox neoliberalism' (Hart 2002:7). Once revolutionaries who swam against the current, they now felt that the only possible response to globalisation was 'to try to catch the wave, to ride the juggernaut' (Lazarus 2004:616).

Policy papers were spun out as consultancies, with many leading neo-Marxists stalking the corridors of power and billing by the hour, were put on lucrative 'retainers' by the new incumbents of power. There was no issue, be it education, welfare or poverty alleviation that could not be turned into a policy document, and swiftly and rationally dealt with as an administrative matter. These challenges were summarily depoliticised in the process of process.

Zola's masses were scripted to leave the stage of history making, to be 'managed' by Faust's technocrats.

The remarkable became routine. Ideals were to be cost recoverable. Activists and former revolutionaries became state functionaries overnight. Everything revolved around order, the New World Order. As the Reconstruction and Development Programme (RDP) gave way to the Growth, Employment and Reconstruction (Gear) plan in 1996, so big business was wooed and that old lightning rod of the rebellion of the 1980s, capitalism, was embraced with great enthusiasm. The ANC government saw foreign investment as crucial to firing up the economy. And so the economy was adjusted to make it attractive to global capital, but instead of investment flowing in, some of the largest local companies decamped and relisted on the London or New York stock exchanges.

As Thabo Mbeki replaced Nelson Mandela as President of South Africa, the government barely made a dent on levels of unemployment and poverty while inequality deepened (Marais 2011:388).

The education system, the great redemption of the island and the great hope of post-apartheid South Africa, has seen well-endowed schools in former white areas opening their doors to those who can pay massive fees, and simultaneously a deterioration of schools in (former) black townships. Zwelinzima Vavi, the general secretary of trade union federation Cosatu, lamented in September 2011 that 'Apartheid fault-lines remain stubbornly in place in our education system. Children born to poor parents remain trapped in an inferior education with wholly inadequate infrastructure … 60% of children are pushed out of the schooling system before they reach grade 12' (Vavi 2011 (a)). Education feeds into existing inequality rather than challenging it.

South Africa is a country of massive forgetting and selective remembering.

Terry Eagleton's words are apposite:

> Many a ruling class has sought to erase from historical memory the blood and squalor in which it was born … It is certain, Hume writes in his *Treatise of Human Nature*, that at the origin of every nation we will find rebellion and usurpation; it is time alone which 'reconciles men to an authority, and makes it seem just and reasonable'. Political legitimacy, in short, is founded on fading memory and blunted sensibility, as crimes come to grow on us like old cronies. So it is that in Britain, France, Ireland and elsewhere, historiographical revisionism in the late bourgeois epoch comes to rewrite the heroics of revolution as the pragmatics of power, in a ceremony of self-oblivion which is not without its neurotic symptomatology. (Eagleton 2002:119)

At what point in the future of our own dispensation will memories fade so that the ideals that motivated our own rebellion, the ideals of equality, non-racialism and democracy, are forgotten and the wielding of power for its own narrow, pragmatic sake is held up as the end of politics itself? At what point will the oldest who 'have borne the most', be seen as but the curiously naïve whose stomachs could not bear the pragmatically, self-enriching smell of rot?

Indeed, already, the progressive erosion of past inequalities through the acquisition of state power has seen the state become the weapon of personal graft and Shakespearean plots for power.

> Vaulting ambition which o'erleaps itself
>
> And falls on th' other
>
> *Macbeth*, Act 1, Scene 7

As the transition unfolds, instead of the ANC dominating the state and bending it into fulfilling the ostensible objectives of redress and redistribution, it has slowly been absorbed into a state beholden to transnational economic forces. 'Rather than the seizure of the state apparatus by the party, what took place was the seizure of the party by the state' (De Oliveira 2006:17). A country that was witness to robust and probing liberal and Marxist debates through the apartheid years has seemingly run out of ideas; 'progress without conflict; distribution without redistribution' (Anderson 2011:12).

The struggle must be written over into one linear narrative of ultimate redemption. Different voices and challenging visions must be eviscerated. Post-1990, Marcus Solomon went to the University of the Western Cape, in which there was:

> this big model of Robben Island, and my daughter asked, Daddy where is your cell? I can't see the section because it was in the dark. The only light was in the single cells. In fact they've reduced Robben Island to the single cells. Yet a lot of the resistance on the island had their origins in the general section and, much as it was trespassed with the violence and brutality of warders and the dogmatism and sectarianism of prisoners, it was also the site of the most beautiful relationships and quest to grow intellectually and politically that cut across organisational boundaries.

So even Robben Island's history must be ironed out so that 'we can have a uniform story to tell' (Kathrada, quoted in Coombes 2003:100). Danny Schechter writes of the impressions of Robben Island's 'younger captives' as 'Mandela University' (Z Space July 18 2011). The debates, the imaginings, the often incredibly different experiences of the island must be siphoned into one person. The island has become a metaphor for the liberation struggle, and so its post-apartheid incarnation becomes symptomatic of the discourse of change.

The ANC, it is asserted, has the 'know-how' to 'master the science and art of forces of crafting long- and short-term common platforms to ensure that all the motive forces pull in the same direction' (African National Congress 2007:12). Barchiesi defines the ANC's approach to 'statecraft, as the objective manifestation of a progressive movement that fuses moral imperatives and technical competence' (2011:254). Alongside a modernist narrative, as Hein Marais shows, the ANC seeks to increase the power of traditional authorities (Marais 2011:425).

> Life's more interesting phenomena, he replied, probably always have this Janus face towards the past and the future … They reveal the ambiguity of life itself.
>
> — Thomas Mann, *Doctor Faustus*

This is the paradox and the power of the ANC. The ability to look two ways at once: modernisation and traditionalism; nurturing the black bourgeoisie and uplifting the poor; African nationalism and non-racialism; anti-imperialism and the most craven genuflection to the International Monetary Fund and World Bank. Right now, *this* ANC is personified in the figure of Jacob Zuma, who straddles the urban and rural, the traditional and the modern, the Robben Islander who can draw on revolutionary credentials to demand 'discipline', 'patience', and 'sacrifice' in the present.

The strains inside the ANC alliance, despite the most plaintive calls to discipline and obedience to the party line, grow. 'Uneasy lies the head that wears the crown', Shakespeare tells us of the usurper Henry IV. As the ANC gears up for its leadership battle once more, Zuma scans the ranks for potential challengers, finding it increasingly difficult to hold the middle ground, cutting an increasingly Macbethian figure:

> Having become King officially by killing Duncan, he (Macbeth) finds that he has achieved nothing: there is always another step to be taken before he is *really* king, secure in his role, and each step taken undoes what he has won because each step breeds more destructive consequences. He is not allowed to become what he is, to be authentically, king; he spends all his time and energy in consolidating his position. (Eagleton 1967:132)

Hamlet's 'tragedians of the city' have risen sporadically and spontaneously. Their rebellion is written in the most romantic and heroic of fashion. But these once militant struggles, if not siphoned into the labyrinth of the state machine, have flattered only to 'melt into air'.

The militant local level protests that calls for service delivery and conscientious councillors almost always end with the President paying a fleeting visit. In scenes reminiscent of Caliban giving allegiance to a new master, 'How does thy honour? Let me lick thy shoe', the people pledge to vote one more time for those that they think can provide the possibility of a better life. Inevitably, the Leader is shocked by what he sees, promising change from on high within the confines of policy. Everything becomes reduced to Foucauldian notions of governmentality, 'the emergence of political rationalities, or mentalities of rule, where rule becomes a matter of the calculated management of the affairs of each and of all in order to achieve certain desirable objectives' (Rose 1996:134). Calculation comes from getting the right research. It is as if policy is evacuated of ideological content and political will and so the 'relationship between data collection, definition of the common good, and policymaking become linear, straightforward, uncontroversial' (Barchiesi 2011:254). Progress gets measured by growth, productivity, efficiency and above all by the ratings of financial agencies, the litmus test of the investment climate.

Those who rebel seek not to transgress and imagine a new world but to be courted. One of the reasons for this is that the elaboration of formal institutions of negotiation and the expansion of rights, act as a container. Civil society resistances have been most often scripted in terms of establishing rights claims and when successful they are announced as significant advances for justice. They have become the first port of call for many social movements and there is very little critical engagement with the ability of social movements to change the balance of power. This strategic (principled?) stance has permeated even those movements that make the most militant claims about their reliance on the power of the masses and their ability to 'live' history outside and beyond the state.

Still, as the limits of rights claims mediated through the courts become more apparent so new subjectivities arise that strain against the boundaries of 'governmentality'.

There are other limitations though.

The organised working class, that old shibboleth of the left, has to contend with a vocal black middle class, a huge young unemployed mass, and the creation of jobs that are casualised and outside formalised bargaining forums. Franco Barchiesi has argued provocatively and persuasively that participation in the labour market is not the route out of poverty. This, he argues, has led to 'the politics of workers' melancholia' for the kind of 'decent jobs' that capitalism simply no longer provides (Barchiesi 2011:255).

The Left, outside the ANC alliance, while adept at critiquing the neoliberal turn, has found it difficult to present alternative ideas to the shaping of economic policy, innovative organisational forms, and a language that fires up the imagination beyond *anti*-privatisation, *anti*-eviction. The social movements' demands and victories around free basic services and free access to anti-retroviral AIDS medicines were impressive but ultimately, instead of threatening the economic system as radical reforms would, they were readily incorporated. While there is an almost reflexive antipathy to 'vanguardism' – the Leninist view of communist or socialist political parties and their leaders 'representing' the 'masses' – there is very little sense of how groupings struggling for the semblance of bare life will overcome sectional and organisational chauvinisms.

In the face of this though, the 'small' rebellions across the country point to the makings of a generalised social implosion because the present arrangements are unsustainable, and the memories of what was promised are still raw. The often brutal suppression of community protest is indicative of a government that has run out of ideas, that tinkers with 'new growth paths' while bemoaning their impotence in the face of global forces. This impotence is summed up memorably by Trevor Manuel, a key Minister in the governments of Nelson Mandela, Thabo Mbeki and Jacob Zuma:

> I want someone to tell me how the government is going to create jobs. It's a terrible admission but governments around the world are impotent when it comes to creating jobs. (Manuel, quoted in Marais 2002:92)

Marxists are fond of saying that every generation sets itself new tasks. Well, every new generation sets itself new targets. As early as 1992, Nelson Mandela warned: 'we are sitting on a time-bomb … Their (poor people's) enemy is now you and me, people who drive a car and have a house. (Their enemy) is order, anything that relates to order' (Saul 2002:41).

Pallo Jordan argues that national liberation movements have embarked on retreats 'in order to prepare for a more coherent and better planned advance' (Quoted in Magubane 2004:658). There has been nothing to indicate an economic policy emerging under the Zuma Presidency that spurs advances to mitigate deepening inequality and provide the much touted windfall of jobs (Vavi 2011 (b)).

Is there a way out? And if there is where will the spark come from? Or is it as many of the Players in the Shakespearean tragedy of our history have pointed out, it is really blood that is compulsory.

THE PLAYER:[25]

We're more of the love, blood, and rhetoric school. Well,
we can do you blood and love without the rhetoric, and
we can do you blood and rhetoric without the love, and
we can do you all three concurrent or consecutive. But we
can't give you love and rhetoric without the blood. Blood
is compulsory – they're all blood, you see.

GUILDENSTERN:
Is that what people want?

THE PLAYER:
It's what we do.

120

GUILDENSTERN:

What will happen after the blood?

THE PLAYER:

It is only then thinking can start, ideas can flow.

121

The Lighthouse on Robben Island.

NOTES

1   One of the reasons for the PAC's formation was what people such as Sobukwe saw as the overdetermining influence of the Communist Party of South Africa on the ANC in the 1950s.

2   Dingake finished three degrees on the Island: BA, BAdmin and BComm.

3   The researcher engaged in a series of conversations with Venkatrathnam between February and May 2011.

4   Apdusa grew out of a split in NEUM. Its first national conference was held in April 1962 and I B Tabata was elected president.

5   'At last, the Bard of Robben Island' in *The Daily Telegraph*, 11 May 2006.

6   In 2002, Leftwich wrote an article in *Granta* entitled 'I Gave the Names'. It speaks to his experiences of giving evidence against his comrades.

7   Daniels interviewed in April 2011.

8   Mkalipi interviewed in April 2011 and June 2011.

9   Cooper interviewed in June 2011.

10   The quotes in this chapter are taken verbatim from the author's interview with Mdingi in March 2011 and June 2011.

11   Masondo remembers the handkerchief incident as part of an earlier incident. They threw a petrol bomb at the home of one of the teachers who they found out was collaborating with the security police. The person who dropped the handkerchief with the initials R. L. was Rex Luphondwana. According to Masondo, he owned up quickly, protecting the others and was given a sentence of five years (SADET 2008:252). What the incident did was to place a particular focus on the Andrew Masondo unit. Masondo's account of the capture centred around the fact that he was worried about the footprints he left behind after a successful operation. 'Some of these young people that were from Pretoria were staying in my backyard. I remove my shoes, because I suspect the shoes will be a problem. Instead of taking the shoes and throwing them away, however, I give them to one of these chaps and say he must go and give them to another chap. The police intercept him. This is how we got arrested in March 1963' (SADET 2008:253).

12   Kathrada interviewed in April 2011.

13   Mac Maharaj remembers the three peasants as having been jailed for killing a headman. He names them as Baba Mvulane, Baba Batane, Tausand (O'Malley 2007:179).

14   'Boerewors' is a sausage and 'Jan Pierewiet' is a mythical Afrikaner character celebrated in song (a *pierewiet* is a joker, a humourist or a clown). Mayat's use of 'Boerewors en Jan Pierewiet liedjie' in this context refers to the attempt by Afrikaner nationalists to create an inward-looking culture insulated from British and local Black trespass.

15   The young man was Tokyo Sexwale (2004:304).

16   Solomon interviewed in March 2011 and June 2011.

17   Gazo interviewed February 2011 and July 2011.

18   Mkunqwana interviewed in February 2011 and July 2011.

19 Makana (or Makhanda; Nxele), a venerated Xhosa warrior, was incarcerated on Robben Island after a defeat at the hands of the British in 1819. He tried to escape by boat but drowned.

20 He was head of Robben Island from 1977 to 1982. Former post-apartheid South African Minister of Justice Dullah Omar, who legally represented many Islanders before 1994, argues that while Harding's approach 'was to win people over, co-opt them … the ANC people who exploited that were aware of his strategies, but were at the same time prepared to play along and gain whatever concession they could' (quoted in Buntman 2003:137). On the other hand, there were accusations that Harding favoured the ANC over other formations. This would make sense if the ANC, unlike the BCM, seemed to buy into Harding's strategy.

21 Isaacs interviewed in February 2011 and June 2011.

22 Masemola, a member of the PAC, was to be transferred to the single section cells. There, together with the help of Mac Maharaj, he successfully made a key that could open cell doors. He was released together with Walter Sisulu and other prisoners in 1989.

23 Sizani interviewed in March 2011 and August 2011.

24 Alexander interviewed in June 2011.

25 With apologies to Tom Stoppard (1967).

The Mosque on Robben Island.

REFERENCES

Ackroyd, P. 2010. *A Brief Guide to William Shakespeare: Without the Boring Bits*. London: Robinson.

Alexander, N. 2011. 'Race is skin deep, humanity is not'. *Cape Times*, 5 April.

ANC Education Department. 1994. *A Policy Framework for Education and Training*. Johannesburg: African National Congress.

Anderson, P. 2011. 'Lula's Brazil'. *London Review of Books* 33(7), 25 March:3–12.

Babenia, N and Edwards, I. 1995. *Memoirs of a Saboteur: Reflections of My Political Activity in India and South Africa*. Belville: Mayibuye Books.

Barchiesi, F. 2011. *Precarious Liberation: Workers, the State and Contested Social Citizenship in Post-apartheid South Africa*. Pietermaritzburg: University of KwaZulu-Natal Press.

Benjamin, W. 1968. *Illuminations*. New York: Knopf Doubleday Publishing.

Bennett, A. 2007. 'The Uncommon Reader'. *London Review of Books* 29(5), 8 March:11–23.

Breytenbach, B. 1984. *The True Confessions of an Albino Terrorist*. Johannesburg: Taurus.

Bryson, B. 2009. *Shakespeare*. London: Harper Press.

Brutus, D. 1968. *Letters to Martha and Other Poems from a South African Prison*. London: Heinemann.

Buck-Morss, S. 2010. 'The Second Time as Farce … Historical Pragamatics and the Untimely Present'. In *The Idea of Communism*, edited by C Douzinas and S Žižek. London: Verso:67–80.

Buntman, F. 2003. *Robben Island and Prisoner Resistance to Apartheid*. New York: Cambridge University Press.

Chisholm, L. 1991. 'Education, Politics and Organisation: The Educational Traditions and Legacies of the Non-European Unity Movement, 1943–86'. *Transformation* 15:1–25.

Connelly, K. 2008. *The Lizard Cage*. London: Vintage Books.

Couzens, T & Willan, B. 1976. 'Solomon T Plaatje, 1876–1932: An Introduction'. *English in Africa* 3(2):1–39.

De Oliveira, F. 2006. 'Lula in the Labyrinth'. *New Left Review* 42:5–23.

Dick, A. 2007. 'Censorship and the Reading Practices of Political Prisoners in South Africa, 1960–1990'. *Innovation* 35:24–55.

Dingake, M. 1987. *My Fight Against Apartheid*. London: Kliptown Books.

Distiller, N. 2005. *South Africa, Shakespeare and Post-colonial Culture*. New York: The Edwin Mellen Press.

Eagleton, T. 1967. *Shakespeare and Society*. London. Chatto & Windus.

Eagleton, T. 2002. 'Capitalism and Form'. *New Left Review* 14:119–131.

Everett, B. 2008. 'Shakespeare and the Elizabethan Sonnet'. *London Review of Books* 30(9), 8 May.

Fadiman, A. 2007. *At Large and at Small: Confessions of a Literary Hedonist*. London: Penguin.

Fanon, F. 1967. *The Wretched of the Earth*. Harmondsworth: Penguin.

Feuntes, C. 2005. *This I Believe*. London: Bloomsbury.

Fukuyama, F. 1992. *The End of History and the Last Man*. New York: Free Press.

Gelb, S. 1999. 'The Politics of Macroeconomic Policy Reform in South Africa'. History Workshop at the University of the Witwatersrand, Johannesburg 18 September.

Gerhart, G. 1978. *Black Power in South Africa: The Evolution of an Ideology*. Berkeley: University of California Press.

Gevisser, M. 2007. *Thabo Mbeki: The Dream Deferred*. Johannesburg: Jonathan Ball Publishers.

Goodson, I. 2006. 'The Rise of the Life Narrative'. *Teacher Education Quarterly*. Fall. 7-21

Hart, G. 2002. *Disabling Globalisation: Places of Power in Post-apartheid South Africa*. Pietermaritzburg: University of Natal Press.

Hofmeyr, I. 2006. 'Reading Debating/Debating Reading: The Case of the Lovedale Literary Society, or Why Mandela Quotes Shakespeare'. In *Africa's Hidden Histories: Everyday Literacy and Making the Self*, edited by K Barber. Bloomington: Indiana University Press.

Isaacs, S. 2010. *Surviving in the Apartheid Prison*. London: Xlibris Publishing.

Johnson, D. 1996. *Shakespeare and South Africa*. Oxford: Clarendon Press.

Kathrada, A. 2008(a). *Memoirs*. Cape Town: Zebra.

Kathrada, A. 2008. *A Simple Freedom*. Johannesburg: Wild Dog Press.

Lazarus, N. 2004. 'The South African Ideology: The Myth of Exceptionalism, the Idea of Renaissance'. *The South Atlantic Quarterly* 103(4):607–628.

Lewin, H. 1976. *Bandiet: Seven Years in a South African Prison*. Harmondsworth: Penguin.

Lewin, H. 2010. *Stones Against the Mirror: Friendship in the time of the South African Struggle*. Cape Town: Umuzi.

Lodge, T. 1985. *Black Politics in South Africa Since 1945*. Johannesburg: Ravan Press.

Lodge, T and Nasson, B. 1991. *All, Here and Now: Black Politics in South Africa in the 1980s*. Cape Town: David Philip Publishers.

London, J. 1944. *The Iron Heel*. Harmondsworth: Penguin.

Mafumadi, T. 2001. *Raymond Mhlaba's personal memoirs*. Pretoria and Cape Town: HSRC Press and Robben Island Museum.

Magubane, Z. 2004. 'The Revolution Betrayed? Globalization, Neoliberalism, and the Post-Apartheid State'. *The South Atlantic Quarterly* 103(4):657–672.

Mandela, N. 1994. *Long Walk to Freedom*. Randburg: Macdonald Purnell.

Marais, H. 2001. *South Africa Limits to Change: The Political Economy of Transformation*. Cape Town: University of Cape Town Press.

Marais, H. 2011. *South Africa Pushed to the Limit: The Political Economy of Change*. Cape Town: University of Cape Town Press.

Maslen, R & Schmidt, M. 2008. *The Shakespeare Handbook: The Bard in Brief*. London: Quercus.

Meer, F. 1988. *Higher than Hope: The Authorized Biography of Nelson Mandela*. London: Hamish Hamilton.

Modisane, B. 1986. *Blame Me on History*. Craighall: AD Donker.

Mogoba, S. 2004. Stone, Steel and Sjambok: Faith on Robben Island. Johannesburg: Ziningweni Communications.

Nash, A. 1999. 'The Moment of Western Marxism in South Africa'. *Comparative Studies of South Asia, Africa and the Middle East*, Vol. XIX Number 1:66–81

Nixon, R. 1987. 'Caribbean and African Appropriations of The Tempest'. *Critical Inquiry* 13:557–578.

Nkosi, L. 1983. *Home and Exile*. London: Longmans.

Orkin, M. 1991. *Shakespeare against Apartheid*. Johannesburg: A.D. Donker.

Orwell, G. 1969. *Inside the Whale and Other Essays*. Harmondsworth: Penguin.

Pamuk, O. 2007. *Other Colours*. London: Faber and Faber.

Plaatje, S. 1982. *Native Life in South Africa*. Johannesburg: Ravan Press.

Pogrund, B. 2009. *How Can a Man Die Better: The Life of Robert Sobukwe*. Johannesburg: Jonathan Ball Publishers.

Rose, N. 1996. 'Identity, Genealogy, History'. In *Questions of Cultural Identity*, edited by S Hall and P du Gay. London: Sage Publications:128–150.

SADET (South African Democracy Education Trust). 2008. *The Road to Democracy: South Africans Telling their Stories. Volume 1 1950–70*. Pretoria: Unisa Press.

Said, E. 1994. *Culture and Imperialism*. London: Vintage.

Sampson, A. 1999. *Mandela: The Authorised Biography*. London: Harper Collins.

Sampson, A. 2008. *The Anatomist*. Johannesburg: Jonathan Ball Publishers.

Sandwith, C. 2011. 'Civility in Question: Cultural Debates in the Non-European Unity Movement'. Paper presented at History Seminar Series, Department of Historical Studies, University of KwaZulu-Natal, 21 September.

Saul, J. 2002. 'Cry for the Beloved Country: The Post-apartheid Denouement', in *Thabo Mbeki's World: The Politics and Ideology of the South African President*, edited by S Jacobs and R Calland. Pietermaritzburg: University of Natal Press, 27–51.

Saul, J. 2008. *Decolonization and Empire*. Johannesburg: Wits University Press.

Schadeberg, J. 1994. *Voices from Robben Island*. Randburg: Ravan Press.

Shakespeare, W. 1965. *William Shakespeare: The Complete Works*. Edited by Peter Alexander. London: Collins.

Scholes, Robert. 1989. *Protocols of Reading*. Yale: Yale University Press.

Sher, A. 2006. 'At last, the Bard of Robben Island'. *The Daily Telegraph*, 22 May.

Sisulu, E. 2004. *Walter and Albertina Sisulu: In Our Time*. Cape Town: David Philip.

Stoppard, T. 1967. *Rosencrantz and Guildenstern are Dead*. New York: Grove Press.

Sustar, L & Karim, A. 2006. *Poetry & Protest: A Dennis Brutus Reader*. Pietermaritzburg: University of KwaZulu-Natal Press.

Trewhela, P. 2009. *Inside Quatro: Uuncovering the Exile History of the ANC and SWAPO*. Johannesburg: Jacana.

Vahed, G & Waetjen, T (eds). 2009. *Dear Ahmedbhai Dear Zuleikhabehn: The Letters of Zuleikhabehn and Ahmed Kathrada (1979–1989)*. Johannesburg: Jacana Media.

Venkatrathnam, S. 2002. 'Voices of Resistance', UKZN (interview), Documentation Centre, University of KwaZulu-Natal.

Vavi, Z. 2011(a). Speech to the South African Democratic Teachers' Union (SADTU) Eastern Cape Congress, 28 September.

Vavi, Z. 2011(b). Keynote address to the South African Catholic Conference of Bishops, Justice and Peace Annual General Meeting. Cosatu press release, 26 February.

Venter, S (ed). 2005. *Ahmed Kathrada's Notebook from Robben Island*. Johannesburg: Jacana.

Wieder, A. 2008. *Teacher and Comrade: Richard Dudley and the Fight for Democracy in South Africa*. Albany: State University of New York Press.

Woledge, E. 2006. 'Interview with Sonny Venkatrathnam'. *Shakespeare at the Centre*, Volume 4.

Wolf, M. 2008. *Proust and the Squid: The Story and Science of the Reading Brain*. Cambridge: Icon Books.

Zwelonke, D M. 1989. *Robben Island*. Oxford: Heinemann.

less, free, unthra...
unclassed, tribeless, And
...pt from awe, worship, degree, t...
himself; just, gentle, wise;
...scious less? — no, yet free from gu...